CONSUMER
OR CONSUMED?

CHARLOTTE **SCANLON-GAMBILL**

Abundant Life Publishing

© Charlotte Scanlon-Gambill 2004

Abundant Life Publishing
Wapping Road, Bradford
West Yorkshire BD3 0EQ

Unless otherwise stated, scripture quotations are from the Holy Bible, New International Version, Copyright © 1973, 1978, 1984 International Bible Society, published by Hodder and Stoughton.

First Published in 2004

Printed by:
Interprint Creative Solutions
Market Flat Lane, Knaresborough
North Yorkshire HG5 9JA

www.interprint-ltd.co.uk

British Library Cataloguing in Publication Data
A catalogue record for this book is available from the British library

ISBN 0-9538516-2-1

DEDICATION

I dedicate this book to my Dad.

From the age of twelve when I first showed a passion for God's House, you have nurtured me and invested your wisdom into my world. You have lavishly poured your love, generosity, laughter, strength, encouragement and friendship into my life. My life is indebted to you. I cannot find enough words to express my love and gratitude.

This book stands as a testimony, for every parent and leader, to the power of empowerment. You have not just empowered me to live my dream but also a whole generation. Dad, you are stuck with me! I will live out my days building God's House alongside you.

'Where you go I will go, and where you stay I will stay. Your people will be my people and your God my God.' (Ruth 1:16)

Thank you

Charl X

THIS BOOK STANDS AS A TESTIMONY
TO THE POWER OF EMPOWERMENT

ME & DAD

CONTENTS

ACKNOWLEDGEMENTS

When I look at my world, I am constantly amazed at the incredible people I have the privilege of building God's House with. There are far too many to mention by name but you are all the people who are consumed for our House, the Abundant Life Church. This book is about you, your zeal, your commitment and the hours of time you give to building the House of God. You are a joy to lead.

A word of thanks to a few special people:

❖ To my gorgeous husband, STEVE. In you I have found an amazing husband, a best friend and a sold out man of God who shares my zeal for the House. Thank you for choosing to share your life with me. I love you!

❖ To my beautiful mum, GLENDA. I have learned so much from your strength, dignity and inner beauty that radiates through your life. You are kind to all you meet, a true reflection of the Father's heart. Thank you for believing in me.

❖ To my dearest friend, LARA. We met in the House, have grown in the House and now we are living our dream in the House. You make my days brighter and my life taste sweeter. You are the friend I asked God to give me, a friend for life.

❖ To STEPHEN AND KAY MATTHEW, faithfulness and loyalty personified. Thank you for encouraging me, for believing in me and helping me to flourish. Our House wouldn't be the same without you.

❖ To HANNAH JOWETT. All those hours sat staring at the screen have produced this book! Your enthusiasm has been infectious. Thank you for your zeal and dedication. And SIMON DEMPSEY, you make me smile. Your giftedness has never been put to better use than here in God's House. We make a great team.

❖ Finally THANK YOU TO ALL who have allowed me to include their story in this book. You have shared your 'fleece' with the world; you make God smile.

"I HAVE GONE FROM A CHILD IN THE HOUSE
TO A WOMAN

FROM A SPECTATOR
TO A SERVER

FROM A VISITOR TO A DWELLER

FROM A CONSUMER TO SOMEBODY TOTALLY CONSUMED"

FROM A FOLLOWER
TO A LEADER

CHAPTER 1

CONSUMER OR CONSUMED?

For as long as I can remember, church has been a part of my life. As a young girl I was always excited about going to church because to me it was an incredible place. From an early age I would go and sense this amazing energy and presence. I felt safe, loved, and at home in God's House. I have been blessed because, from the day I was born, my parents took me to church and I've been in the same church all my life. It has gone through many changes and so have I. We have grown up and matured together.

The House of God is where I first went to crèche, kid's church, youth club and young adults. It's where I auditioned to be in my first drama, where I sang publicly for the first time in a choir. It's where I first served as a volunteer in the church coffee shop. It is where I met my life long friends who are still in the same church with their own families now. It's where I met my husband, where we got married, where we learned to build our lives together and where we had our baby girl dedicated. It's where I learned to dream.

You may think I have led a sheltered life but I don't look at it like that. I was privileged to grow up around men and women of God and learn from their wisdom from an early age. If it was good enough for Jesus, who spent his early years learning in the House of God, then it's good enough for me.

I believe the House of God is the best environment to raise children in but many parents and children have become just attendees rather than dwellers in the House. I look at our church and watch as families join for the first time. They enter as a family and their children's young eyes widen as they try to take in all the activity. The lights, the music, the huge TV screens, the lively choir, and the young guy rapping on stage. The 'Starbucks style' coffee shop with its outdoor terrace. The skateboard park and the floodlit football pitch. This is before they have even seen the kid's church with bouncy castles, play stations, and the children's band and choir. I watch as each member of that family starts to get plugged in to the House. With around 170 ministries to choose from, it's not difficult to find something that excites and interests them!

I look at the teenagers who are working in the media department doing graphic design and operating TV cameras, or who are helping in the catering team or working as a steward setting up the building and patrolling the car park. Others are in the band learning to play with other musicians or fine-tuning their vocal ability at the choir rehearsals. They are out helping in the community, feeding the homeless and touching hurting lives with the practical love of God. No wonder the local schools want to send their pupils to our church for work experience; they have recognized that our House is a great environment for training the next generation. In fact we have better facilities and equipment than many of the places the kids get sent to, and the teachers know that here their pupils will be well looked after.

I have gone from being a child in the House to a woman, from a spectator to a server, from a follower to a leader, from a visitor to a dweller and from a consumer to someone totally consumed. My husband and I want to raise our daughter in God's House, I want her to see a community of people who are making an impact in their lifetime like her Mum saw when she was growing up. To that end I would encourage every parent to read this book so that every child under their care can become ignited with the same love for God's House, a love we must pass down the generations.

God's House is my absolute passion. I am a self-confessed, seeking no cure, churchaholic! It enthuses my spirit, inspires my creativity and gives my life purpose. I have fallen in love with God's House and I want you to know about the awesome place that it is, and can be in your local church and community. Maybe you have just started reading this book and are thinking, 'I don't see those things in God's House here and my church doesn't have all those ministries.' Well, I want to challenge that thinking and get you to ask yourself, 'why not?' Why can't the House of God where you are based be a place of excellence, a place that is exciting and full of creativity? It all starts with just a handful of people becoming consumed by the House and you will be amazed what a difference you can make. So read on, be inspired and fall in love all over again with the House of God.

CONSUMED OR CONSUMER?

There are two types of people in God's House, the consumers and the consumed. To be consumed means 'to be fully absorbed; to be devoured completely; to be eaten up; for you to disappear because you have been swallowed by something bigger'. When you are consumed there is nothing left of you. If I consume a glass of water, the water is still there but it's inside me. Being consumed by the House of

God is like that; you can't separate the two. Your needs and desires become less important than the big picture of what God's House is about. It is no longer there just to meet your needs but to point a dying world to an incredible Saviour.

Consumers are defined in the dictionary as 'people who go to a place for the sole purpose of getting what they need.' And many Christians look upon God's House like that. They sit in meetings thinking, 'That didn't do much for me tonight,' or 'That didn't answer my situation,' or 'They didn't talk about marriage tonight and I really needed help in my marriage.' You can be in the presence of God and have so much on your mind, that you are completely taken up with those difficulties. It means you sit through awesome worship giving God a list of what you want him to do. You are thinking, 'God, can you sort this situation out for me?' and 'You haven't forgotten about that person who let me down badly the other day have you Lord?' or 'You do know that this is happening in my life right now don't you?' Meanwhile God is saying, 'for goodness sake, I am not Father Christmas so put your list away.' We've got to stop going to church as consumers, coming with a list of needs and then acting like a spoilt child if we don't get exactly what we want.

You can tell the difference between consumers and consumed people in the way they respond to God's House. Consumers can sleep in and miss church but consumed people would get out of their sick bed to be there. Consumers will listen to those who criticise the pastors and the leaders of the House but the consumed will stop it and change relationships. Consumers do not volunteer to serve but the consumed serve at everything. Consumers only see their own needs but the consumed see the needs of others. Consumers ask 'What do I have to do?' but consumed people don't need to be asked. They just get on and work. Consumers will not turn up to a meeting because they don't like the speaker, or because they've heard that message before. Consumed people will come to give their support even if they have heard the same message ten, twenty or thirty times before. Consumers can't understand what I am so worked up about! Consumed people feel a passion for God's House which excites them and causes them to live beyond what others think is 'reasonable' in their quest to build God's House!

DIFFERENT APPROACH

I don't know about you but I am a great shopper. I love going to great big malls! But when I go, it is for one purpose – to get what I need. Whether it is another pair of shoes or a new lipstick, I am there to shop until I drop! But when I come to the House of God I approach it with a totally different mentality. I don't go to shop, I go to serve God, love and exalt him. I go to dwell in his House. But sadly, for many the House of God is like a trip to the shopping mall where they have their favourite stores, which they want God to bless their lives through, and then they leave and get on with the rest of their week.

Your approach to God's House is very important. When an aeroplane comes in to land, its approach to the runway will determine the success of the landing. In the same way our approach to life and our approach to God's House will affect our landing. Many people are not enjoying the House because their approach is wrong. How do you approach God's House? The chances are you haven't even thought about it. It's just another responsibility in your already overcrowded schedule. Do you approach as a lodger who just goes to the House but does not linger or dwell there? You simply visit and pay your rent in the offering bucket every week. Or maybe you approach the House as if you are doing God a favour by being there and making an appearance. Or do you approach with fear and trembling because, for you, the House is a place of tension and criticism? And you're the pastor!

If the answer is 'yes' to any of the above, your landing will not be a safe, smooth or enjoyable one. It will be bumpy and turbulent; you may even need to brace yourself for a painful impact that's heading your way!

Ecclesiastes says: *'Guard your steps when you go to the house of God.'* It then goes on to give advice on how to make a good approach. *'Go near to listen, rather than to offer the sacrifice of fools who do not know what they do wrong. Do not be quick with your mouth, do not be hasty in your heart to utter anything before God.'* [1] The Message Bible puts it this way: *'Watch your step when you enter God's House. Enter to learn. That's far better than mindlessly offering a sacrifice, doing more harm than good. Don't shoot off your mouth, or speak before you think. Don't be too quick to tell God what you think he wants to hear. God's in charge, not you – the less you speak, the better.'*

In other words we should approach with a listening ear and a guarded mouth. When I have approached to listen I have always learned a lot more than when I have approached with a list. Maybe I need to remind you that God knows everything. He is omnipresent, almighty, all-sufficient, the great 'I Am'. He knows what you are facing today, what you will face tomorrow and what you will face next year. He has been ahead of you and is not in a panic, so why waste your time in the House telling him what he already knows? Ecclesiastes encourages us to think before we speak and if we just thought for a moment about the awesomeness of God then we would approach his House consumed.

Don't misunderstand me, I am not saying that to approach God's House in the right way you must enter in silence. That certainly wouldn't work in our House! Sunday mornings are crazy. Getting ready in time, putting our baby girl in the car before she needs another nappy changing or brings her breakfast back up on what's already her second outfit that morning. I'm sure all parents know what I mean! Neither is it about behaving in some religious or legalistic way before you go to church. The change in your approach starts with a change in your perspective, the way you see the House. We need to see God's House as our home; it's where I was born to dwell. It is not a hotel, it's not a halfway house and it's certainly not a shopping mall. When we start to see God's House differently then our approach will change no matter how chaotic our lives get.

DIFFERENT OPINION

Consumers and consumed people have a completely different perspective on life and often do not understand each other. I can recall several conversations where this difference has stood out because I was a consumed person talking to a consumer.

As a young teenager I remember once sharing my dream with someone of one day working full time in God's House and serving my Dad, who was the Pastor. I knew that he was pouring his life into building an incredible House for God and I wanted to be a part of it. They told me I needed to go out into the world, build a career and find my own identity. They implied I was trying to play it safe by wanting to work with my family. Looking back, that conversation could have sent me one of two ways. Either to the Job Centre to review my options, or make me more determined to pursue my dream. Thankfully I chose the latter and now realize I was being advised by a consumer. That person came to church but gave their life to pursuing their career and now their children are doing the same and have left the church to pursue riches and status on the career ladder.

When my husband Steve and I got married one of the leaders in the church came to us with some marital advice saying, 'now that you're getting married, you need to take a year out together and not do anything in the church, just build your marriage.' He even gave us scriptures to back it up and I'm sure he had our best interests at heart. Do you know what? That would have driven us crazy! We would have been violating what God had called us both to do! We would have sat at home looking at each other, saying, 'Are you bored?' 'Yeah. Are you bored?' 'Yeah, let's go to church.' 'OK then.'

In our first year of marriage we had a blast and not only grew more in love with each other but also prospered as we served together. We also made a difference to the world around us by working for something bigger than ourselves, the vision of the House.

Again I remember when I announced we were expecting our first child, some of the consumers in the church advised that now was the time to take a break from work. They said I needed to slow down and not be so committed to the House. It appeared to be sensible advice but it just didn't sit right with Steve and I. As a couple we asked God and other consumed people for guidance. We wanted to be great parents but didn't want to step back from being involved in the House. I said to God, 'Which do you want me to be? A full-time mum or serve and lead in your House?' His reply was, 'What do you want?' If you live your life consumed for the House, God will often ask you what you want because he knows that your desires will be in line with his desire for your life. The scripture says, *'Delight yourself in the Lord and he will give you the desires of your heart.'*[2] So I said, 'Well God, I want to do both. I want to have my cake and eat it!' And God said, 'fine!'

Within a few weeks of making this decision my sister, Esther, agreed to work for us as our nanny and my life at the office became more organized with the arrival of my new assistant Shirley. I returned to work a few weeks after Hope Cherish was born. When she was just six weeks old, I hosted our annual women's conference Cherish, and had the privilege of blessing the lives of hundreds of women through that event. Some thought I was completely crazy! They don't understand me, but God does!

Hope is now one year old and is a happy, contented baby who loves being in the House. She enjoys the music and lifts her hands in the meeting, copying all the people around her. Neither Hope or I are missing out, there is simply a grace in God for me to do all that I do in ministry. God sees it and there is a 'smile' on it, energy for it and an anointing on it, but some people simply can't understand it.

As a consumed person my passion for God's House makes me go beyond what some people think is reasonable. It is the consumers who sit there and say, 'she needs to slow down, she needs to calm down!' When people try to give you advice always check the source of the counsel. Ask yourself whether they are a consumer or a consumed person because each approaches life with a completely different mindset to the other.

When Job was going through his time of testing, the consumers in his world were more than forthcoming with advice. His wife told him to *'Curse God and die!'* But Job responded from a consumed heart saying, *'You foolish woman, shall I accept only good from God and not trouble?'*³ In other words Job was saying, 'I will not treat God like a consumer expecting him just to dish out what I need. I am consumed with passion for him and if that means going through these trials and tests, I will do it. I am not quitting!'

Be careful that consumers don't advise you in a way that will make you compromise on what God has said. Check the conversations you have using this measuring line and it will help you decide whether to act on that advice or ignore it.

Conversations like the ones I had take place in the House all the time and we must learn how to handle these potential conflicts of interest. I was told to stop dreaming and get a career, and if I had followed that advice I might not have been sitting here living my dream and writing this book. I thank God for the amazing wisdom my parents gave me when they told me to go for my dream. They weren't frightened I would miss out on a great career by putting God's House first, they knew that as I delighted in God and his House, my desires would become a reality. It saddens me when kids tell their parents they want to arrange their world around the House of God by taking a year out to attend our Leadership Academy or serve as a volunteer, and their parents throw cold water on it. It is the best foundation they can lay! I am so grateful that I was not directed that way because I would have missed out on helping to build our House here at the Abundant Life Church. I would have missed seeing the gospel reach into well over a hundred nations through our TV programmes and media publications. I wouldn't be organizing events for people from all over the world to come and learn more about God or have the privilege of standing on platforms to inspire more people to follow Christ. I am very aware that without other consumed people encouraging me to go for it and not settle for the status quo, I might not have done all this. If you want good advice, ask a consumed person.

If I need wisdom I ask my family and closest friends who are consumed for the House. Together we are part of a new generation of believers who don't have to do what everyone else has always done. We approach life, friendship, marriage and parenting from a consumed perspective, and change what in the past has just been accepted as the usual way of doing things.

[1] Ecclesiastes 5:1
[2] Psalm 37:4
[3] Job 2:9-10

SISTER   DAUGHTER   FRIEND   MOTHER

WE APPROACH LIFE, FRIENDSHIP, MARRIAGE AND PARENTING
FROM A CONSUMED PERSPECTIVE

BROTHER   FATHER   HUSBAND   FRIEND

CATH'S STORY

'When I walked through the doors of the Abundant Life Church for the first time, I remember thinking to myself, I'm home.'

I had the best childhood ever! Growing up with my Mum and Dad, three brothers and three sisters was one big adventure. Fun and laughter filled the house and there was never a dull moment! I was blessed with two amazing parents who loved each of us unconditionally and instilled some great principles into our lives.

When I was 16 years old I discovered the world of 'adult life' and boy, was it different! I remember sneaking out with my mates to a nightclub and thinking, 'this is fantastic!' This 'adult world' was so different to my home life. It was glamorous, glitzy and everyone appeared to be having a good time. People looked cool, wore trendy clothes, drove posh cars, lived in very nice houses and had lots of friends. I threw myself into it wholeheartedly and life became a never-ending party.

But all parties come to an end and ten years on I was the mother of two young children and in a relationship with their father that was going downhill fast. Life had carried me to a place I never intended to be and it wasn't how I had imagined it would end up.

I still had lots of dreams for my life but they seemed unreachable. But despite this, having them at least kept me going when times were bad. I would close my eyes and ears to the chaos I was in and pretend it wasn't happening, just like a child would.

Then one day I met a really enthusiastic Christian who talked to me about God. I had heard much of it before from my upbringing. Then he asked me straight out: 'Do you have peace and a relationship with God? It just freaked me out and I thought he was crazy! As he left he said, 'You can ask God into your life anytime and anywhere.'

But what he said wouldn't leave me because I didn't have peace and my life was a complete mess. I longed for the peace he spoke about. So one day after taking my kids to school, I locked my front door and cried out to God saying 'God if you can give me peace like this guy said, I'll give you a go.' And that was the beginning of my life changing radically.

When I walked through the doors of the Abundant Life Church for the first time, I remember thinking to myself, 'I'm home'. The thought caught me by surprise because it was an unfamiliar environment and I did not know anyone. But I was really overwhelmed with a feeling of, 'I'm home'.

Nine years on, I love my life and am a really blessed woman! I have my wonderful natural family around me, and my church family who are the most amazing people ever.

God has entrusted me with two fantastic, gifted children. At fifteen, Nicole is a confident, beautiful, young lady, who loves God and his House. My son Jonathan was once so disruptive his school wanted to exclude him but is now a talented, funny and handsome fourteen year old who is fully involved in the life of the church. I thank God for them both.

I am now living the dreams I had for life. I have always wanted to work with hurting and abused women to help restore hope and dignity to their lives. Although I left school with no qualifications I am now the Manager of an amazing Housing Project which provides accommodation to vulnerable young people. It equips them with the skills they need to help them live independently and build a better life.

Recently I was driving home with my daughter and sister in the car, and in the midst of the laughter and chatter I just thought to myself, 'I am a successful woman.' Successful, not because of what I have, but simply because of who I now am in Christ. It is through God's unconditional love in my life, and my amazing God Centred, Purpose Driven and People Empowering church, that I am prospering in every area of my life.

Sometimes I pinch myself and think how on earth did I get here? I believe things are as they are in my life because years ago I made a choice to stay planted in God's House and serve. I served wherever there was a need and let God mould and shape me along the way. Things have not always been easy but God has been faithful to me. God is now using all I have learned on the journey so far as I raise my family, do my job and serve in his House. He is so good!

Cath

Cath Miller

ELAN | JOJO | DOLLY

LOVING HIS
HOUSE

"WHEN I THINK OF THE ZEALOTS IN OUR HOUSE
I THINK OF A HUGE RANGE OF PERSONALITIES"

SUPERJOCK
CRAZY IN HIS HOUSE

CHAPTER 2

ZEAL FOR THE HOUSE

T his is a serious issue we are dealing with. The treatment of God's House is not something we can ignore or take lightly. Once Jesus went into his Father's House and found it filled with consumers. His response was not a casual one. In fact, many were shocked at how severely Jesus dealt with those in the House that day.

'*After this he went down to Capernaum with his mother and brothers and his disciples. There they stayed for a few days. When it was almost time for the Jewish Passover, Jesus went up to Jerusalem. In the temple courts he found men selling cattle, sheep and doves, and others sitting at tables exchanging money. So he made a whip out of cords, and drove all from the temple area, both sheep and cattle; he scattered the coins of the moneychangers and overturned their tables. To those who sold doves he said, "get these out of here! How dare you turn my Father's house into a market?" His disciples remembered that it is written, "Zeal for your house will consume me."*' [1]

Jesus was appalled! These people were in God's House for one purpose only, to exchange their goods. And sad to say, there are things going on in God's House today that we need to get upset about with a similar righteous zeal. We need to say, 'Enough is enough.' We need 'zeal for the House' to consume us. Right now you may be afraid to challenge or confront people who have a bad attitude towards God's House. But when godly zeal consumes you, words come out of your mouth that you didn't plan to say. You get the courage, inner strength and determination to deal with situations that you couldn't deal with before.

THE FILTER OF ZEAL

Zeal for God's House is a great filter. It helps you articulate what needs to be said with passion and yet this passion is filtered by your love for the House. So instead of retaliating purely from your own human emotions, your zeal for the House is stronger than your annoyance with that person or situation. It enables you to smile, even if it is through gritted teeth, at that person you would like to give a piece of your mind to because of the trouble they have caused. Your love for the House is greater than your desire to retaliate. When we don't use this filter, we start to do things we regret. We must make decisions that spring from our righteous zeal and not from our frustration. This is especially important for those leading God's House because the decisions they take in times of conflict could not only damage the individual concerned but also have the potential to damage the whole House.

I have learned so much from being under Pastor Paul's leadership. There are many times when people have treated him wrongly and I have thought, 'you should tell the church what they just said! Tell them how awful that person is and everybody will support you.' Instead, he has chosen to show great grace and not mentioned a thing. Why? Because zeal for the House consumes him and his heart is to see people restored in the House, not damaged. Looking at situations through the filter of righteous zeal always helps you to look beyond the hurt of a situation and rescue the life of the person involved.

WHERE ARE THE ZEALOTS?

David said, *'zeal for your House consumes me.'*[2] The Amplified Bible puts it this way, *'zeal for your House has eaten me up.'* I like that phrase! *'Zeal for God's House has completely eaten me up.'*

It's important to stop for a moment and define what zeal actually is. Many people have a wrong understanding of this word and think a zealous person is an extrovert. They think it is someone who is always in the limelight, motivating and urging people to be as outgoing as they are. They would not consider that someone of a quieter disposition, who is more comfortable working in the background than they are up front, could ever be a zealot. But when I think of the zealots in our House, I think of a huge range of personalities. More often than not they are quite happy if they are never noticed, because they are not seeking attention or a 'moment of glory'; their passion is to see the bigger picture fulfilled.

The quiet guy who serves in the car park every week, come rain or shine; the retired couple who give up their time to visit and pastor the next generation; the young people who go out every week feeding the needy in our city; the single mum who gets up early to catch three buses just to get to church and greet people on the door; the young people who turn down weekend jobs because they refuse to work on a Sunday and miss church – all these are the true zealots of church life. So before you look for the loudest, most enthusiastic people to find your zealots, think again. Instead, seek out the faithful members of the House who are there every week, consistently serving, whether they are noticed or not.[3] People like this are consumed by a zeal that needs no outward impetus.

Zeal is a God-breathed source of supply that will get you out of bed even when you don't feel like it! Building God's House is hard work but if you try and do it out of obligation or your own enthusiasm, you won't make it. Only having an all-consuming zeal will keep you going. There are so many people in our church who are my heroes because zeal for this House has consumed them. I don't have time to mention them all because this book isn't long enough, but here is a glimpse of a few of their lives to demonstrate what this zeal looks like.

Tim is in his early twenties and is one of the youngest bank managers in the country. He has a massive amount of responsibility. When we have conferences on at the Abundant Life Church, he has been known to go into work at four o'clock in the morning to do his paperwork at the bank and sort out the duties for his staff. He plans his work schedules and attends to everything he needs to so that he can be back at church for 9.30am to welcome people arriving in their cars. Nobody makes or asks him to do it. It's just what people do when they are fuelled by zeal for the House.

Derek is a chef in our church. Sometimes when we are hosting guests he cooks supper for us. He then goes home and works in his kitchen until 2.30am baking scones for the church coffee shop! And, he is still in church for the morning service.

Sonia used to manage our coffee shop as a volunteer and is now part of our full-time staff. She is a single mum and would travel in with her little boy, early in the morning on the bus, and sometimes cycle ten miles from Leeds, just to set up the coffee machines. When that was done she would go into the band rehearsal, as she is also part of the choir. After the rehearsal she would be back in the coffee shop serving and afterwards stay behind to help tidy up and sort out staff rotas. She is consumed with zeal for this House!

These are just a few examples of what happens when people are passionate about God's House. Their lives speak the language of zeal. As the Psalm says, *'better is one day in your courts than a thousand elsewhere.'*[4] People like these would rather be doorkeepers in the House of the Lord than get paid thousands of pounds a year for running a bank, but are willing to do both. They would rather be doorkeepers in the House of the Lord, than stress out about being a single mum and bemoaning how hard life is! They would rather be doorkeepers in the House of the Lord and lay down their lives for something far bigger than their own personal agendas. Zeal for God's House consumes them and they are my heroes.

These people are not 'one offs' and they don't all live in Bradford. The truth is, they are in every town, every city and are in every church. Many go unnoticed and others are overlooked. More often than not, many have yet to find a practical way of expressing their zeal. But it is time for every zealot to come out of the closet and just start building somewhere, anywhere!

In another of his Psalms David says, *'one thing I ask of the Lord, this is what I seek: that I may dwell in the House of the Lord all the days of my life.'*[5] Just 'one thing' he asked, not twenty or even five things. That's the only thing he asked for! If you could ask for just one thing right now, would you ask to dwell in the House of God forever? Or would that be the last thing you would want? If you had to dwell, twenty-four hours a day in the House for the rest of your life, would that be a nightmare for you?

DILUTED ZEAL

Many of these potential zealots in the House have diluted their zeal down in order to comply with the status quo of church life. The strength of their passion intimidates people around them, so they end up apologising for it and they trade in their zeal for something weaker. These are the people who sit in the meeting desperate to 'Amen' the preacher and start a rapturous round of applause as he shares his heart for the House. But they look around and think they are alone. So they decide that a nod of the head will suffice. I want to say to every nodding church member, let out the 'Amen' and start the applause because you might just find that you are not alone.

Sometimes these 'closet zealots' sit in church thinking, 'If I told them my dream for this House they would think I had lost the plot.' Sadly, many leaders have left the blueprint for the House they once dreamed of building for God on the shelf, gathering dust. They are too scared or feel they are outnumbered by consumers, and simply don't have the energy to try and communicate their passion for the House to people who are more interested in their own house than God's.

If your Pastor announced that there was going to be two services a week instead of one, what would your reaction be? Would you be there, supporting this venture and new growth opportunity, or would you rather be at home having a cup of tea and putting your feet up? Do you encourage people who are passionate about God, or do you pour cold water on their enthusiasm and wish that they would calm down and stop being so 'over the top' all the time?

Many reading this need to stop diluting their zeal and take up the challenge. It's time to stop apologising and start telling it like it is. As a leader I have had to learn that some things are not negotiable. You cannot surrender your vision for the House in favour of everyone else's opinion and approval. You just have to start building. And you'll be amazed at what happens! God will bless you, he will prosper you and people who are of like heart will find you. Those who are consumed by the House of God will find you.

Not only will they find you, they will want to help serve and bless your world in every possible way. They are drawn by your zeal and want to serve you so that you can keep doing all that you are doing. They become like David's mighty men who went to great lengths just to get David a cup of water because they loved his all-consuming zeal for God.

Another expression of this is seen in the fact that when you take care of God's House, he takes care of yours. This has become an increasing reality in my own life. It came home to me again in our recent house move. I returned from a trip to Australia to find a whole host of practical details for me to arrange including walls to paint, curtains to hang, boxes to unpack and on top of all that a first birthday party to organise for Hope. Yet within three days everything had been taken care of. An army of volunteers came and served our family without me having to beg and plead for help. In fact in the end I was turning down offers of help as we already had enough willing hands, from Tom who came straight from work to help paint walls, to Matt who spent two days hauling rubbish to the tip and Michael who hung enough light fittings to illuminate the neighbourhood. The list goes on. Amidst the chaos of my house move I was overwhelmed with the heart of those who had come to help, who just wanted to bless and serve us. It reminded me again that when you put God's House first your own house be taken care of too.

GOD WANTS A HOUSE NOT AN APARTMENT

Notice that David didn't say 'zeal for my ministry', or 'zeal for my agenda'. It wasn't 'zeal for my victories' or 'zeal for becoming a famous king'. His zeal wasn't for what God could do for him or for the people he liked. It wasn't even 'zeal for God' alone but 'zeal for God's House', the whole thing. I have often noticed that people are consumed by or passionate just for their particular area of God's House. When this happens we end up building God an apartment block instead of a House and you can guarantee that there will be fights between the neighbours! Somebody plays their music too loud, so you have to go upstairs and complain. The equivalent of this goes on in church.

I'm thrilled that you're consumed by the worship ministry and are passionate about having awesome worship in the House. But I'm not thrilled if you go to the back of the hall and sit chatting with your friends after you've 'done your thing' on stage until the band get back up on the platform again! That is just not good enough and shows that you are only in love with one room in the House. We need hearts that say, 'if I don't get to do my bit on stage tonight I don't care, because I'm not consumed by my bit. I'm consumed by what's best for the House.' David was a musician but he didn't say, 'zeal for the music room' or 'zeal for being in the presence of the musicians consumes me.' He said, 'zeal for the House.' That means the basement, the cellar, the attic, the living room, the lounge and the bathroom. It includes every room in the House.

When our youth department had some money donated a while ago, they used some of it to buy equipment for the boardroom, a room which they rarely use. Why? Because they had a zeal for the House that extended beyond their area and they wanted to bless other departments of the church with their money, even though they could have used it themselves. It's a picture of how the House should be with everybody helping each other, and loving each others rooms as much as their own.

TEACH YOUR KIDS TO SHARE

A growing church is like a family that keeps having more children. Suddenly little 'Jessica' who previously had your undivided attention realises that she no longer has a monopoly on your cuddles, or a special place reserved on your knee. By the time sibling number four or five arrives she realises that her relationship with Mum and Dad has to change. Jessica is just as important to her parents as before but has had to learn that the needs of the other children in the family are just as important as hers.

This is what happens in a growing church. Before our church increased in size, each department could get time with me, or one of the other senior leaders whenever they wanted. If the youth department wanted to use the minibus they could, because no one else ever needed it on a Friday. But growth changes things. Now when the youth need the minibus, so do the community action teams and the family centre. The youth department who never had to queue before are now in a line with others whose needs are just as valid. The worship team who always got to use the main building whenever they needed it for rehearsals now find that the youth band, kids choir, drama team and dance ministry all need the same venue. And so we could go on!

New additions to a natural family may not have been planned for by the other siblings, but they were planned by the parents of the House. It is now up to the children to adapt, move over and make room for the new additions. The same is true in the church. The kids pastor may not have planned to share his space with the arrival of yet another ministry but God, the Father and owner of the House did plan for them. And he's looking for a zeal in his House that says it may be a squash but there is always room for one more. Being part of a growing church means your household has to learn to share.

One of the first things we taught our daughter was to share. From the age of five months you could ask her to share and she would hand over her most precious possession, her bottle of milk! Sharing is something we have to learn because it doesn't come naturally. Over the years I have had many 'Groundhog Day' experiences listening to the same conversations from different departments. 'But Charlotte, we have always used the bus on Tuesdays, everyone knows that, and I went to get it this week and someone else was using it. It's not fair!' They had of course booked it but the long-time users had just taken it for granted! ' Charlotte, we set the room up just as we wanted two days ago and now another ministry have put their equipment in and taken over the space for a meeting today.' And so I could go on.

As leaders we have to realise that an element of this will always exist inside a growing House. Make sure that no department starts to mark out its territory and then becomes confrontational or defensive when they are later asked to share resources. We have had to teach our staff on numerous occasions about the bigger picture and lay down some house rules to help everybody get along. Simple things like putting equipment back where you found it and making everyone fill in a booking form for certain items or a purchase request form if they want to buy something. No department is given preferential treatment and all their needs are given equal consideration because each room is just as important.

These are some of the dynamics involved when you are building God's House because it has to become a home for such a large and diverse family. If one department manages to get their own way all the time and operates outside the house rules, you are heading for trouble and at worst maybe even a church split. Always look out for those who are trying to build an apartment in the House and stop it happening. Never put people in charge of ministries who are so consumed by their particular area that they don't care about the rest of the House. We are called to build God a House not an apartment block.

A while ago some of our department leaders came to ask my advice on what to say at their team get-together the following weekend. They were trying to think of a catchy message or a new angle so I said to them, 'Just teach what was said on Sunday. If God's House has one owner and its primary mouthpiece is the senior leadership, then we don't need to try and reinvent the wheel in each department. Take what God is saying to our whole House and apply it to your room of the House.' They did just that and had a great night. It deepened their understanding of how the vision of the House could be worked out practically through their department.

Our church has one vision statement, one mission and every department takes their lead from that. The children hear it in kids church, the youth meetings carry the same emphasis and the worship department reflects the heart and direction of the House in the songs they write. Our teaching team complement one another in what they bring to the church and everyone carries an awareness of what the owner of the House is saying in any particular season. No matter which room you enter in our House you will hear the same message, feel the same spirit and walk away with the same core values.

When people let zeal for the House consume them they throw away their own agendas and instead live by the code of that House. In the natural, if you send your kids to someone's house for tea you hope that they will be good representatives for your family. How they behave at home is now going to have an impact on the house they are visiting. Spiritually we need to have the same confidence, so when we send people out from our House into other spiritual homes, they represent God's House well. We don't want them to take the favour and the opportunities meant for the glory of the House and waste them on their own personal agenda.

Whatever David saw that caused him to say *'zeal for your house consumes me'*, is what I'm seeing and is what we are building here in our city. Now let me take you through the keyhole of God's wonderful House.

[1] John 2:12
[2] Psalm 69:9
[3] Ephesians 6:6-7
[4] Psalm 84:10
[5] Psalm 27:4

"ZEAL IS A GOD BREATHED
SOURCE OF SUPPLY"

TIM'S STORY

'It's not about what those around you think, it's about playing your part in God's House to the full.'

I came to Bradford seven years ago from Northern Ireland for the sole reason of getting a good degree at the University of Bradford. I was reading Management and Technology with the purpose of moving to London or New York once I had graduated.

I arrived at university as a believer, having been brought up in a Christian home but didn't find a good church until well into my second year – which was a complete 'God thing.' I had part-time work at the famous Alhambra Theatre in Bradford and on one particular shift happened to be working with the then Student Ministry leader from the Abundant Life Church. We got talking, he invited me to church and the rest, as they say, is history – I've been here ever since!

A month later, I was asked to help in the Car Park Ministry. My approach to serving in church has always been if a job needs doing, then do it and three months later aged just 19 years I was asked to take on the responsibility for coordinating all the stewarding teams. A short time after that I was asked to take charge of running the Student Ministry in the church and was absolutely amazed at the trust being given to me. I have never taken that trust for granted and count it a privilege and honour that I am able to serve in such an awesome church.

When I finished university I had a number of job offers from around the world to consider but it was no contest - I decided to stay firmly planted in the House I had come to love so much. Making the commitment to stay was a complete step of faith because I didn't have a job to go to in this region.

I trusted God and a few weeks later a major UK bank that I had been working for part time offered me a Business Managers role. I was flabbergasted – or 'gob-smacked' as they say in Bradford! This role usually requires anything up to ten years banking experience before you would be eligible. The person who offered me the job took a tremendous risk as it made me the youngest Business Manager in the UK. Once given the opportunity I was determined to flourish in my role.

It constantly amazes me how my role in God's House has equipped me and I can use the great principles I have learnt there and apply them to my role in the bank. The stewards who serve at church in my teams do so voluntarily, not because they are salaried and I learned there that for people to work as a team, they must have a clear purpose and also have fun doing it. I want everyone on my teams to develop a positive attitude too. I was able to bring all this practical experience of people management into the bank.

For an organisation such as a bank that is built around giving orders, I was and still am a maverick. I challenge staff to live their dreams and I try to make the bank a fun place to be. I was able to get my assistant at church a role as an advisor in the bank and together we are now able to work as a positive Christian influence in the office. I have an amazing opportunity to take biblical principles learned at church and adopt them as practical management tools.

In all that I do both in and out of God's House I want to embody excellence. When I was growing up in Ireland, my father owned a painting and decorating firm. He instilled in me that there is no point in ever doing a rubbish job or leaving a job half-done. So many people volunteer to do things in work or at church but miss that level of commitment to excellence.

Sometimes the only thing we are able to work on in a given situation is our attitude. I want to have a 'can do' attitude in all that I do. It's not about living to impress anyone but God. I don't live for a thank you or praise because sometimes the best feelings are achieved when no one says anything to you and you know that you've done a great job. You only live once and it's forever, so you have got to cram everything possible into your days.

I have often worked at the bank until very late at night after starting at seven that morning and thought nothing about it. My question is why should it be any different when at church? The apostle Paul sewed tents in the evenings and still managed to establish churches, write his New Testament letters and leave a great legacy for us. On one occasion during a women's conference at church I was unable to get the time off work to help oversee the stewarding. So, I started work at 3.30am in the morning to make sure I could get to church for 9.00am. I went back to work after the conference to complete things. The conference went well and I was shattered. It was several months before I even told anyone that I had only had 3 hours sleep each night during the conference. Why? Because it's not about what those around you think, it's about playing your part in God's House to the full.

I truly believe that when you are serving you need to rule over your body, which would often prefer to sit and do nothing. Some churches that I've visited revolve around what I call 'The Bus Journey of church life'. By that I mean people are prepared to get on the bus but only want to be a passenger and not a worker. We must all die to self, put aside our selfish ambition and live a life that is the pure essence of Christ. I know that I'm not a finished gemstone, I still need more shaping but that's only possible as I stay around God centred people who are committed to the same goal of building a beautiful House for God, which will be a light to our community.

Zeal for God's House has consumed me!

Tim Nelson

JUDAH THE
INCREDIBLE HULK

"SOMETHING I LOVE ABOUT ABUNDANT LIFE CHURCH
IS THAT NOBODY LOOKS OUT OF PLACE"

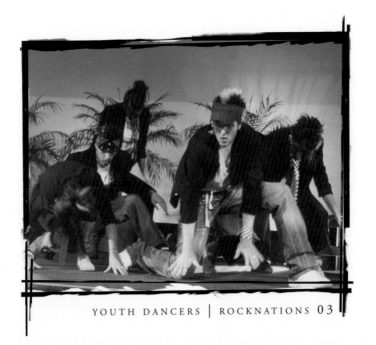

YOUTH DANCERS | ROCKNATIONS 03

CHAPTER 3

LOOKING THROUGH
THE KEYHOLE

H ere in the UK we have a TV show called 'Through the Keyhole' which appeals to the curious and somewhat nosey side of our characters! It gives viewers the chance to snoop around the homes of the rich and famous of our day, from sporting greats to music stars and famous actors. The catchphrase of the show is, 'Who lives in a house like this?' A panel of guests, and the viewers at home, have to work out who lives in the house by looking at their belongings, the décor and even their bed-side reading books. Sometimes the panel guess from the few clues they have seen because the identity of the owner is obvious from even the smallest details of the house. Then other times they have no idea because the celebrity lives a double life. Their public persona is flamboyant, bold and outgoing but their home is understated, far less vibrant and much more traditional than their public image suggests.

When we are building God's House we need to make sure the image we portray of Jesus through our advertising, spoken word and witness measures up to the expression of Jesus they will find in the House. If someone came along and took a 'sneaky peek' through the keyhole of your church, what conclusions would they draw about who lives there?

WHO LIVES IN A HOUSE LIKE THIS?

We can easily speak about Jesus, his beauty, compassion, and heart for the lost; his limitless love, his forgiveness that is freely given and his immeasurable generosity. We rightly present an irresistible Jesus! His House is therefore irresistible too. But if the people who heard us speak about this Jesus, go to where he is supposed to live and end up confused by what they find, they will conclude that Jesus must be living a double life. If they cannot find anything that matches the Jesus they have heard about in his House, there is a problem. It is as if they look through the keyhole and are asked 'Who Lives in a House like this?' and the last person that ever springs to mind is Jesus Christ.

Looking through the keyhole of some Houses you see a place of stress not of peace, a place of bitterness rather than forgiveness. You try to locate compassion and patience but instead find yourself falling over intolerance and impatience. A peek through the keyhole of some Houses reveals a very dysfunctional family. There is friction, infighting, gossip and an overwhelmingly bad atmosphere. This breaks God's heart. He looks down from heaven and cries out, 'This is not what my House is supposed to look like. I don't own that. I don't recognise those ugly furnishings. They don't belong to me!' From looking at some houses you can only conclude that the owner must be lonely, broke and miserable. The house is cold, stark and filled with people who look like they don't want to be there.

But when you look through the keyhole of God's real House you see very different furniture. You will find footstools of faith, pillows of peace, trophies of grace, ornaments of mercy, cabinets of love, pantries full of wisdom, rooms full of laughter, corridors full of friendship, ovens full of blessing, fridges full of forgiveness and every room filled with the all-pervasive aroma of Christ. It is time to hold a mirror up to our churches and examine the reflection we are giving to those around. If we are to build awesome churches that will touch our communities, cities and the world, we have to know what God's House really looks like. So, let us now take a look through the keyhole of God's House to discover what key characteristics should be there, to ensure that no one is left wondering who the owner is.

A PLACE OF BELONGING

I once saw a video about the work Pastor Tommy Barnett and his son Matthew do through the Los Angeles Dream Centre. It's an incredible ministry which reaches people in downtown LA. It exists to give them a second chance. The programme featured a young man sharing his testimony at a large gathering of pastors and leaders. He told them how he ran a large ministry which was feeding and clothing the homeless in the city of LA. He spoke of his work with drug pushers and gang members and how every day he was seeing lost people find a place they could call home. As the leaders applauded his efforts to make a difference, he continued to share his own story. He explained how he used to be a transvestite living on the streets of Los Angeles and how his life had been in a downward spiral of drugs, prostitution and violence. Then one day he walked through the door of the Dream Centre and found not just a message but a home, a place of belonging. It extended its love and inclusion to him. This was somewhere he felt accepted, even though when he arrived he was dressed as a woman.

It was easy to cheer on the efforts of this young man from the other side of his transformation but the question he asked the leaders that day brought me to tears. He said, 'Would you have let me come as I was to your church?' He didn't get saved and change his ways over night and for many weeks he went to the House as a transvestite but he was still made to feel like he had come home. The staff at the Dream Centre loved him all the way through his process of change and helped him work out his salvation a day at a time. There was no drastic overnight change but he was still given a place to belong. Would that be OK in your House?

You see, God's House was always meant to be a place of belonging for all people, whether you like it or not. God doesn't want your opinion, he just wants your co-operation. I am so glad that someone let me belong.

Something I love about Abundant Life Church is that nobody looks out of place! You can be there wearing your latest Gucci or

Armani designer outfit and sit next to somebody wearing a bin liner held together with safety pins who has spiky 'mohican' hair. We have policemen sat next to ex-offenders and politicians sat next to people from some of the poorest housing estates in our city. Yet everyone belongs together in the House of God! Now where else in society can you find that?

God's House should always be a place of belonging for everyone, no matter what their age, race, background or status in life. You can have the young sat next to the old, the rich next to the poor and the black sat next to the white - and it all makes sense. The scriptures say, *'How lovely is your dwelling-place, O Lord Almighty! My soul yearns, even faints, for the courts of the Lord; my heart and my flesh cry out for the living God. Even the sparrow has found a home, and the swallow a nest for herself where she may have her young - a place near your altar, O Lord Almighty, my King and my God. Blessed are those who dwell in your house; they are ever praising you.'* [1] Even the sparrow and swallow find a place to nest in the House! God's House is meant to be a place where all can find a place to dwell and belong in the presence of God.

REACHING ALL KINDS

We get all types of people coming through our doors but in some churches, everyone looks the same and talks the same. You only need to look at creation to see that God loves variety! He filled the earth with all types of creatures as an expression of who he is and his House needs to be the same. When Noah was told to build an ark it was to accommodate every type of animal, not just the ones Mr and Mrs Noah particularly liked or thought were clean enough to make good boat pets. He was told to make a place of belonging for the cute donkey and the not so cute spitting camel! If your church has only one type of person, it is likely you will only reach that kind and fail to express the wonderful diversity that is in God's heart.

Several years ago at Abundant Life Church our 'type' was mainly white, middle class people and the journey we made has been well documented in Pastor Paul's book 'Crossing Over'. Some of our people were simply not willing to make the transition and it started a barrage of phone calls and letters to the leadership team from people who were just not prepared to come to church and risk sitting next to a prostitute or drug addict. In the end we simply had to say, 'it is a shame you feel like this about the people we are bringing to church, but this is not going to change.' We had committed as a leadership to build God's House and fill it with every type of person we could possibly reach. We had to decide not to give in to those who wanted to keep the House for themselves, their friends and family.

I clearly remember Pastor Paul standing up one Sunday and saying, 'If you don't like sitting next to a prostitute or a homeless person, then I'm sorry but we need your seat!' You may think this sounds harsh but when you are consumed for God's House you will not settle for compromise any longer. There are just too many people in your city who are spiritually homeless and unless God's House flings its doors wide open, they will stay homeless.

It took us time and a lot of patience to reach other types. But when you are consumed for the House you don't see what separates people but what unites them. You are building an awesome, glorious House for God who extends his love and grace to all people. He is abundant in every way and we need to build a House that reflects this.

Is this the type of House you are building for God? Can the vulnerable, the hurting, the refugee and the disenfranchised find belonging there? Do you embrace both rich and poor, male and female, both black and white, young and old? Can famous people like actors, pop stars, footballers and others who have immensely successful, high profile careers, call your House their home? This is the House we must build.

To do this we need to have a House that has an overflow of life and love to give away. Sadly many people who come to church, hoping to find answers to their problems leave after finding the cupboards are bare. They find famine in the House instead of the abundance of life, joy, wisdom, faith and peace that should be there.

We have got to build Houses that are so abundant that we can help fill every demand placed on us. There should be no person coming that we can't love or reach out to.

The Psalm says, *'They feast in the abundance of your house; you give them drink from your river of delights.'*[2] At your church, do you freely give all that you have to people. Can anybody come and get an abundance of love even if you don't have the financial resources or manpower to help that situation right now? A smile doesn't cost anything for you to give, but to the person on the receiving end who thought no one cared for them, it was a miracle. For them the House suddenly became a place of belonging.

A PLACE OF SAFETY

God's House should be a place of safety for all who come. Some people who came to our House arrived nervous and suspicious, unsure of what they would find. Our job was to make them feel safe. We have even had people come who were literally on the run in fear for their lives; people who had left the religion they were born into and now faced a death threat if they were caught anywhere near the House of God. Yet these same people are now living and dwelling in God's House, the nightmares and the panic that used to keep them awake at night have disappeared as the environment of the House makes them feel safe again. David describes God's House as a place of safety, he said, *'One thing I ask of the Lord, this is what I seek; that I may dwell in the house of the Lord all the days of my life, to gaze upon the beauty of the Lord and to seek him in his temple. For in the day of trouble he will keep me safe in his dwelling; he will hide me in the shelter of his tabernacle and set me high upon a rock.'*[3]

Are you building a safe House, one where people in need can find a safe dwelling? Or is your House in turmoil all the time and the last thing you feel is safe? Some churches are like entering a war zone. People arrive for a service with their Bible in one hand and a hard hat in the other, just in case there's any falling 'rubble'! Does your church have factions and departments that are not at peace with each other? In wartime, if you are killed by friendly fire, it means that someone on your own side shot you. The point is, the bullet will still do the same amount of damage to you as if it was fired by an enemy. People will not feel safe if they are constantly worried about being hit by 'friendly fire.' Those you are trying to reach don't want to come to church with a hard hat and protective clothing. They don't want to feel mishandled or abused but safe in God's House.

SAFE HOUSES HAVE ORDER

When we say that God's House should be a place of safety, it means more than just being a place of refuge for the hurting and a sanctuary for the mistreated. The word 'safety' also means creating a place of order. Something I thank Pastor Paul for is the way he has made me feel safe as an ordinary member of our church. He has built a House where we have order that creates a safe environment. I have been to several churches and sat through meetings with a sense of panic and fear at what was coming next. There were numerous words of prophecy that anybody could seemingly give over the microphone, endless words of knowledge, mind boggling visions, long winded prayers and clown-like entertainment at half time. I have sat in meetings feeling pressured by the preaching, which was judging me rather than nurturing me and I certainly did not feel safe. In fact I was left with the impression that this House existed for the members to do their own thing, not God's thing.

Our meetings used to be very different to how they are today. Before, you didn't want to risk bringing your friend from the office in case someone got up and said something embarrassing, which did happen on several occasions. Also, you couldn't really expect them to sit through a three-hour church service on their first visit. It was really difficult to explain to them why some people were babbling in a 'foreign' language, and why others would suddenly decide to start shaking and fall on the floor.

When we crossed our church over several years ago, this gave us the opportunity to bring some order to the House and get rid of the baggage that wasn't helping anybody. Our meetings went from three hours to one and a half hours, we moved from endless contributions from random individuals to focused worship, led by our worship pastors. The preaching of the Word was left for those who knew what God wanted to say to our House and was not a chance for people to try out their latest message. The Word was preached by the consumed; it was full of wisdom and you could apply it straight to your life with no need for added explanation. Our church became ordered, cringe free and safe.

Your House will never have order if you don't make some decisions about what is allowed to happen there. Our people find great safety in the fact that they don't have to wade through the confusion of everyone else's opinions but can clearly hear the direction for the House through the leadership team. It also means we don't have just anybody come and minister in our House. We have learned to protect our pulpit and not offer it as a platform for anyone to abuse. Our pulpit is only entrusted to those who are consumed for the House and are practising what they preach in their own church.

A SAFETY THAT IS TANGIBLE

Your House also needs to be safe in every room. This safety is both spiritual and practical. In our House we want you to feel safe when you enter our premises. You are surrounded by a great security team, your kids are watched by workers who have all been police checked and every child is registered for their safety. Even your car is safe as our car park team keep an eye on it while you are in the House. This is practical safety and spiritually we go to the same lengths. You will be safe under the teaching, safe under the counselling team, and safe in the worship. This is tangible safety. Are people safe in your church? Is your House one of order or do you need to start to deal with the chaos you have been praying God would take away?

If you belong to the House, you have to deal with it just as any natural homeowner is responsible for the safety of their own home. They cannot blame the neighbours for a lack of diligence in protecting their property if they are broken into. Equally we cannot blame God if there is chaos in our home. We have to roll our sleeves up and bring some order. We have to build a House that is a place of belonging and a House that is a place of safety for all people.

[1] Psalm 84:1-4
[2] Psalm 36:8
[3] Psalm 27:4

CATHY- RUNNING OUR FAMILY CENTRE
A PLACE OF SAFETY FOR FAMILIES IN NEED

"GOD'S HOUSE SHOULD BE A PLACE OF SAFETY
FOR ALL WHO COME"

A SAFE PLACE
TO RAISE THE NEXT GENERATION

NICOLA'S STORY

'I couldn't take anymore and decided to kill myself. At that moment I remembered what I'd learned in God's House'

As a teenager I was abused and ended up drifting from one unhealthy relationship to another through a need to feel protected. I began drinking to fit in with the 'in crowd' and ended up taking speed, ecstasy and eventually became a heroin and crack addict. I had two young sons who were both taken from me because I was considered unfit to look after them. Over this ten-year period I had two nervous breakdowns and ended up on medication for depression and schizophrenia. I didn't see my children for months at a time as the drugs completely took over my life.

I was so ashamed of what I'd become and what I'd let happen to my children. Everywhere I went I looked at the floor and not into people's eyes so they couldn't see what a bad person I was.

One day, a friend of mine who was a prostitute told me about some women from The Abundant Life Church who went out into the 'red light' area of Bradford and gave the girls tea, coffee, food and told them about God. She said there was something different about them. Eventually I met them myself and had to agree that they were different. I was completely lost and they seemed to know exactly who they were and what I needed to do for my life to change.

Some days I would find bags of shopping outside my front door, left by these girls because they knew that I hardly ate. Then one day they invited me to church. I was sure I would hate it because I thought church wasn't for people like me, it was for perfect people who had it all together. But I really liked it! In fact it overwhelmed me. I didn't understand it all but I just felt loved and accepted. I knew it was a safe place to be.

I would often go down to the church to get food and clothes because I knew the people there genuinely cared about what happened to me. They gave me hope and I was baptised later that year.

I was still very messed up at this stage and as a result made some bad choices. I ended up going back to my partner of ten years and ended up back on heroin. Things declined rapidly. I was put on medication and I withdrew from society. I became a prisoner in my own mind, tormented by my own thoughts and the shame and guilt I felt. I went to bed crying and woke up crying because I was still alive. I thought there was no way out and that I deserved to be so unhappy because of what I'd allowed to happen to me and my children.

Weak and tired, I couldn't take anymore and decided to kill myself. At that moment I remembered what I'd learned in God's House; that God loved me and there was another way. Out of sheer desperation I threw myself on the floor and cried, 'God, if you really do exist, I need you to help me or I'm going to die!' I found some inner strength and went to ask for help. Just one week later I was in a rehabilitation centre.

That was three years ago. I have now been clean from all drugs and medication since that crisis moment. My life has been completely transformed and restored by God's love for me. I have been shown how to live God's way. I have had my thinking renewed through God's Word and the amazing teaching we have here at Abundant Life Church. I have learned so many things I never knew before, things that I can use in my life every day as I become a bigger and better person. Life with God is fun, exciting and I feel empowered as a person. I love God so much and love being in his House with other people who love him like I do.

My boys are now 16 and 14. The youngest has been with me for two years now. The great thing is that they have all the information that I never had. They are surrounded by wisdom in God's House and are being shown a different way to live their lives.

In God's House my dreams have been ignited again and I am now sharing that discovery with others. I love people because I know how much God loves them. God's people showed me his unconditional love and it saved my life, and I am now compelled to show it to others. The Bible says those who have been forgiven much, love much (Luke 7:47). I reckon that's why I love God so much and find such fulfilment in showing his love to others.

Today I know who I am and where I am meant to be. For the first time in my life I have found the real me. I'm a daughter of the Most High God, planted in his House, showing his unconditional love to the world he loves so much.

Nicola

Nicola Phelan

"LAUGHTER IS INFECTIOUS
AND IT ENRICHES YOUR LIFE
IT ACTUALLY BRINGS HEALTH TO YOUR BODY"

FI- YOU'RE PRICELESS!

CHAPTER 4

LISTENING THROUGH THE KEYHOLE

When we look through the keyhole of God's House we shouldn't only see a place of belonging and safety, we should hear certain sounds. The House of God has its own distinct sound. What noises are drifting through the keyhole of your House?

Have you ever had noisy neighbours? You may never have had the opportunity to meet them but the sound that comes from their house tells you more than you may ever find out in an introductory conversation. The family next door may look like they are all together, Mr and Mrs Perfect with their two perfect children. But the noise coming from their house of the husband and wife screaming at one another, the children slamming doors in anger and even the dog joining in, tells a different story about life in that house.

We recently moved into a new home. After only being there a few hours we suddenly heard a sound. It was drifting through the windows of a house across the street. We hadn't even seen our new neighbours yet but we had just found out that one of them was a practising drummer. This went on for several hours every day for the first week until one day we saw an older gentleman complaining at their front door. My husband, who is a fellow drummer, went over to offer the reprimanded teenage boy some advice on how to quieten down his drum kit. While he was there, the man who had gone to complain explained that the noise had carried all the way down the street to his home ten houses away. The sound of your House travels, and whether you like it or not, people know what is going on inside your House by the sounds that are drifting through your keyhole, out of your windows and up through the chimney. Just because you have closed your door and don't think the world can see the dysfunction inside your House, don't forget they can still hear what is going on. You cannot see gossip but you can hear it. You cannot see negativity but you can hear it. You cannot see criticism but you can hear it. We can be so bothered about what people see and totally overlook what they are hearing.

So, what should God's House sound like? What should people hear when they press their ear up to the keyhole of the church? What noises are your neighbours a few doors away hearing? Here are a few of the sounds that let people know, God lives here!

THE SOUND OF WISDOM

'By wisdom a house is built and by understanding it is established and by knowledge its rooms are filled with rare and beautiful treasures.'[1]
If we want our House to reflect its owner, our words and conversations should be full of wisdom.

Before I go any further can I just settle one thing that constantly frustrates me: Wisdom is nothing to do with age! I have met some very unwise older people who in mid-life are still making poor relational and life choices. I also know some very wise young people who are only in their twenties and are making an amazing difference to their world and have achieved incredible things. People have often said to me, 'I don't understand how you can have so much wisdom when you are only 31 years old.' My answer is always that I have learned it by being in God's House. I cannot take any credit for it, other than ensuring I was in the right place. I have been privileged to sit under the teaching and counsel of people who are living a consumed life and they have been generous enough to share their wisdom.

Wisdom is not something that is mystical, hard to grasp or reserved for the very spiritual. Wisdom is a building material and it is needed to build God's House. It is real, it is practical and it is easy to understand. It is the cement that holds the House together.

At Abundant Life we are seeking to hand everyone this building tool. Wisdom is in our preaching, it's in our counsel and in our conversations. The Word you sit under in the House should be helping you lay another course of 'bricks' in your marriage, your family and lifestyle choices. Many times people can use the pulpit to try and impress. They are so heavenly minded in their presentation that it is of no earthly use to people who are desperate for some practical wisdom for their life. In our House we have wise kids and wise teenagers. They are like sponges, soaking up the wisdom around them. Before long you hear them saying things that definitely prove they have wisdom beyond their years.

If you have ever spent a prolonged period of time in another nation, where they speak another language or have a different accent, eventually the sound of your own voice will start to replicate the dominant sound around you. My husband Steve is American but has now lived in the UK for over ten years. During those ten years his accent has started to change. His once very broad American accent has now softened so much that sometimes people mistake him for an Australian or a Canadian, and sometimes even a Yorkshire man. What has happened? He hasn't tried to change his accent, he has just been influenced by the sound of the people he is doing life with. The same is true in the spiritual. When people enter God's House and decide to dwell there, the sound of their voice should start to change. Their speech and their language should increasingly carry the sound of wisdom.

People come into our House all the time from very difficult and dysfunctional backgrounds. They have been raised in a house where the dominant sound was of abuse, foul language and angry exchanges of conversation. However, within a few weeks of being in God's House, the sound of their voice and their language begins to change. With the same mouth that previously cursed God, they are now worshipping and adoring him.

ASK FOR WISDOM

When Solomon was called to a lifetime of building God's House, he asked for wisdom, not provisions or workers. Many people have plenty of these things but they still aren't building God's House right. Wisdom is what will keep your house upright. You have got to wise up if you want to build something great for God. We must constantly keep our ear attuned for the sound of wisdom. That sound can be heard through a CD, a book and from other great Houses around the world. If you are short of wisdom to build your House, go and glean some wisdom from fellow builders in the Kingdom of God. Our team have visited many great Houses across the world to learn from how they are being built.

One of the annual conferences we host as a church is called Stronger and its mandate is to equip and train builders of the House. During the conference, when I look out across the auditorium, it is full of people poised with notebooks and pens who have come to glean wisdom for their House. I stand and applaud every one of them in my heart, because they have decided to make a journey to get wisdom and gain some understanding. They are teachable and willing to sit in the seat of the learner. Their presence in the room is saying, 'We will not reinvent the wheel; we will learn from others.' With this attitude we will get God's House built a lot quicker. Through their search for wisdom they will take away with them truths that they can build on, unwrap and apply to the structure they are building. They are determined to build something that will last.

THE SOUND OF LAUGHTER

The Bible says, *'The One enthroned in heaven laughs.'*[2] God actually sits in heaven and laughs! God has a great big belly-laugh which is heard by all of heaven. So why isn't that sound resonating around every House built in his name? Many people do not associate the sound of laughter and an atmosphere of fun with God's House. They would feel it was irreverent and somehow unholy to have a good laugh in the presence of the Lord! But I don't want to be on a miserable building site. I don't want to live in a House where people look like they are sucking lemons! That type of House will not get me out of bed on a morning. It will make me stay in my own home where I can be myself and have a laugh.

God created humour, he created people who would know how to tell a great joke and have fun together. But often people arrive at God's House and feel they have to behave in a sombre way for them to be accepted and taken seriously. I think that is very sad.

Cathy Ward is an amazing lady in our church. She heads up our Family Centre which helps needy families with wisdom in budgeting, parenting and other life skills. She also has a family of four adopted children to look after. She wrote to me some time ago to say thank you for the sound of laughter in our House and I want to share with you an extract from the letter she wrote:

'I don't know if you have ever noticed in churches how 'reserved, quiet, sensible and calm' people equals 'holy, reverent and spiritual.' And how 'fun loving, outgoing, lively and now and again plain silly', equals immature, irresponsible and severely lacking in reverence. One of the big things I needed to get over when I came to ALC was that I could just be 'me'. Before I had always tried to be 'calm, quiet and sensible' but it didn't work for me – I could never fit into the church handbook definition of 'a spiritual, holy and wholesome woman of God' and I couldn't contain myself long enough to be able to join the club. But you have started a new club with an all-inclusive definition

for the 'spiritual, holy and wholesome' woman of God releasing me and people like me, to be themselves.'

Cathy, like many others in our House, was drawn by the sound of laughter. It saddens me that many people are made to feel they have to apologise all the time for having a sense of humour and being able to see the funny side of life. People need laughter and fun, God created them this way. Laughter is infectious and it enriches your life. It actually brings health to your body and it will bring health to the spiritual body too. *'A cheerful heart is good medicine but a crushed spirit dries up the bones'*[3] says the scripture. Have you ever been outside a room and heard laughter coming from inside? If you are like me, you are desperate to go in and find out what is so funny. Everyone loves to share laughter and it is a sound that will make the person listening at the keyhole want to open the door and enter the House.

I have found that God's House can be such a funny place, because it attracts all kinds of people. The situations you come across and the people you deal with are often hilarious. If you don't fall about laughing at some of the things that happen, you would end up crying. For example, we once had Elvis come to our building! A guy who honestly thought he was Elvis, turned up one day and announced that he wanted to 'sing some songs' in our church because 'Elvis does gospel.' He had on an Elvis belt-buckle, hat and everything!

Another time, when we were just lost in worship as a congregation, in a very 'holy' moment, Sonia, one of our choir members started to look less angelic and more distracted as the song progressed. At that time she was managing our coffee shop and as she was singing, she glanced up to the balcony and saw a guy helping himself to the food from the coffee shop during the worship! She was singing in the choir and at the same time trying to keep an eye on him as he went towards the muffin box - which had the pastor's muffins in for after the service. There he was, scoffing them all as we were worshipping! He then moved on to the freezer and started stuffing tubs of Haagen Das ice-cream into his pockets.

By this time, one of the stewards had spotted him and confronted the man:

'Have you stolen that ice cream?' he asked.

'What ice cream?' replied the man. Meanwhile, chocolate ice cream is starting to run down one leg and strawberry ripple down the other.

'The ice cream in your pocket?' continued the steward.

'Oh, I brought it with me!' he says. Now this is someone who rides to church on our buses! We bring him to the meetings.

So the steward said: 'You're telling me that you got on a bus half an hour away, came to church and then sat through the worship and that ice cream has stayed frozen in your pockets?'

And the guy replies, 'It's my ice cream, I bought it at the supermarket before I came!'

We laughed a lot about that guy and the melting ice-cream. In fact I'm still laughing about it today!

LAUGHTER IS THE BEST ANAESTHETIC

It is a lot easier to sort problems out in the House when you use laughter as an anaesthetic. If people have the anaesthetic of laughter when you need to bring correction or rebuke to their lives, it won't hurt as much when you do the surgery because the wound will be numbed by the anaesthetic. If someone has to address a painful issue in your life, laughter eases the pain. It stops the problems in life overwhelming you and blowing everything out of proportion.

Some leaders have 'sit downs' with their church members that are like pulling teeth without anaesthetic! In the UK, one of the more traditional forms of anaesthetic was known as 'gas and air' but it is rarely used today. It is time for leaders to learn what the 'gas and air ministry' is and give it to people first. We pull a lot of teeth in our church but, as it happens, much of the time those whose lives we are operating on don't realise it. They don't jump in pain or react when they see the surgeon's knife coming towards them, because we have created an environment where the Word, which cuts *'sharper than a two edged sword'*, has been delivered with joy and laughter.[4]

How is the gas and air ministry in your church? Maybe the first person you need to give it to is yourself. My Mum refuses to go to any dentist who will not give her gas and air. She even recently went to casualty to have a splinter removed from her finger but wouldn't let the Doctor go anywhere near her until they had found some gas and air. People in your House will not let you remove the splinters from their lives until you discover the gas and air ministry.

So, how do you put the sound of laughter into your House? In the same way you would in the natural. You don't pray for a sense of humour, you just get one. Start to enjoy the House instead of enduring it and make space in your House to have some fun. When I was growing up our home was filled with the sound of laughter because my parents put it there. We would create times in our day where we would just do crazy stuff. From hula dancing in the front room to sliding down the staircase in a race on our tummies, parents included! We'd play-fight with Dad until one of us got hurt and I still remember Mum shouting up the stairs, 'I told you it would end in tears.' It was great fun!

See the funny side to life. Laugh with your friends, laugh with your partner, laugh with your kids and laugh with those in God's House. Lighten up and learn to laugh at yourself. His *'yoke is easy and his burden is light'*[5] so any yoke that is weighing you down, bending you over and causing your face to frown, does not belong to him. We have got to accept the fact that we are not perfect, we will all make mistakes and from time to time we will mess up. So get over it, look in the mirror and laugh! Let laughter consume you. Let it fill your heart and bring a smile to your face.

A HOUSE OF THANKSGIVING AND PRAISE

'Praise the name of the Lord; Praise him, you servants of the Lord, you who minister in the house of the Lord, in the courts of the house of our God. Praise the Lord, for the Lord is good; sing praise to his name, for that is pleasant.'[6]

This verse is written to those in God's House. If you are in the House you should be making a noise called 'praise'. Praise is not quiet, it is not passive and it is not optional. Have you ever shared a house with someone who likes to play loud music? Recently our very patient Finance Director, Richard, who normally would never ask anybody for anything, came to ask if we would consider moving his office to the other side of the building. When we asked him why, we found out that the sound from the office next door had become so unbearable he could no longer work in peace. He had even gone to the trouble of getting our building maintenance people to insulate his office walls and had resorted, at times, to wearing earplugs before bringing his request to us. But, however hard he tried, he could not block out the sound from next door. The noisy neighbour was Mark Stevens, one of our worship pastors, who likes nothing better than to sit at his keyboard and praise very loudly!

That is what God's House should sound like. It should be full of passionate people praising. No matter what the circumstances, praise is always a great sound to make. Praise will get you through situations quicker and easier. Praise got Paul through being in prison. Job praised God through many difficulties and so can you. Praise is powerful and the sound of it in your House will change people's world. It will lift up their head and help them look and feel differently about their lives.

God likes his praise with thanksgiving. The Psalmist says, *'Enter his gates with thanksgiving and his courts with praise; give thanks to him and praise his name.'*[7] In the natural we want family members who live with us and eat from our table, to appreciate our home and be thankful for it. The same is true spiritually in God's

House. We can sometimes get so busy with the housework that we forget to say 'thank you' to the one who owns the House. Don't get too busy to say thank you.

In our House we are committed to not only praising him but to saying thank you; thanking God, thanking those who lead us and those who are building with us. In our church we regularly take time out to honour people who have blessed our spiritual home. We stop our service to take a moment and tell certain individuals how much we appreciate all they do as they live a life that is consumed by the House. These moments are very powerful, even though all we did was say 'thank you'. Somehow those moments touch our whole house afresh. There is power in thanksgiving and I am sure that every House could stand another dose of thanksgiving. I have never met an over-encouraged leader, an over-thanked parent or an over-appreciated servant in the House. Saying 'thank you' costs nothing but it means everything. When I read the testimonies of the people in this book and consider the hundreds of other lives with equally amazing stories of how the House of God has changed their world, there is no shortage of things to give thanks for. The sound of thanksgiving has the power to strengthen, affirm, spur on, motivate, elevate, dignify, enthuse and restore those who hear it.

Jesus was moved by a grateful heart. In the story of the ten lepers we read of ten lives that had been destroyed by the debilitating disease of leprosy.[8] It was not only physically painful but also caused them to be social outcasts. One day these lepers met Jesus and found him to be a man who wasn't afraid to extend his hand to their disease-ridden bodies and heal them. You would think that after a lifetime of living with the stigma of leprosy, there would not be enough hours in that day to tell Jesus how thankful they were. Yet in the excitement of their new-found freedom, they rushed off to tell everyone their great news and nine of them forgot to say 'thank you' to the one who had made it possible. Only one took the time to express his gratitude. I don't believe the other nine were ungrateful, they were just forgetful, and we can be the same.

Parents are too often aware that the children who live in their house and eat from their table, are not ungrateful for all that's done for them, but they can easily take it all for granted and forget to say 'thank you'. They presume you know they are grateful and therefore don't see the importance of saying the actual words. We need to say 'thank you'. On that day when one of the ten lepers remembered the power of thanksgiving and sought Jesus out to say 'thank you', what happened next is a window into the heart of God. He did not only get healed but he was made whole. He had his limbs fully restored and his body was made completely whole. He drew out of the heart of God an extra touch from heaven. I have discovered a grateful heart moves heaven.

If you want to keep the touch of heaven on your House, keep the sound of thanksgiving in all you do. Sing songs of gratitude, pray prayers of appreciation, testify your thanksgiving, write it and preach it. But whatever you do, don't hide it. Let the world know that this House is a grateful one.

[1] Proverbs 24:3
[2] Psalm 2:4
[3] Proverbs 17:22
[4] Hebrews 4:12
[5] Matthew 11:28-30
[6] Psalm 135:1-3
[7] Psalm 100:4
[8] Luke 17:11

"IF YOU WANT TO KEEP THE TOUCH OF HEAVEN
ON YOUR HOUSE
KEEP THE SOUND OF THANKSGIVING
IN ALL YOU DO"

TIM'S STORY

'Not only has God restored my life, he has taken me beyond restoration to a life that is prospering in all areas as I have remained planted in God's House'

Hi there! I'm Tim, 33 and just married. I have my own business and life is good but it has not always been like this.

I grew up on a council estate in Wakefield in a large family. Money was scarce and things were very tough. My dad was an alcoholic and worked as a bouncer. He would bring this violence home by beating up our Mum and us kids quite often.

I found that hanging around with the gangs was more appealing than hard study and it wasn't long before I started getting into trouble – firstly at school leading to suspensions and then with the police. I left school with no formal qualifications but with the beginnings of a long criminal history.

Within a few months I received a three-year jail sentence for a vicious assault in a gang fight where I came close to killing someone. When I was in jail, none of my so-called mates or gang members came to see me and I remember feeling let down by that. I started dabbling with drugs in jail and I continued being violent to other prisoners.

After my release I continued taking drugs at raves all across the country. I took speed and E's in ever increasing amounts – always looking for a higher high but I only ever felt empty the morning after. During this period my daughter was born but I was so irresponsible and caught up in the drug culture, that I walked out of her life and didn't see her again for many years.

I started dabbling with heroin, which quickly turned into a habit. This was a drug that I always said I'd never take. But my head was so done in that not thinking straight I succumbed to smoking it at first and then turned to the needle. Things deteriorated so badly that I started selling heroin to fund my raging habit. The more I sold, the more I injected, the more I injected the more I sold – selling thousands of pounds every day on the streets and injecting myself up to ten times a day. I would also smoke crack and dope yet still needed sedatives to help me sleep.

My criminal lifestyle accelerated and I sank even lower and ended up mugging people, robbing, burgling and beating people up for money. I was a physical and emotional mess, underweight, my veins had collapsed and I just wanted to die.

It was at this time someone told me that there was a God who loved me despite the mess I was in. This freaked me out! I thought these people were on more drugs than me! But I did begin to wonder if there was any truth in what they were saying. So I decided to find out if this God that people raved about was real. I went to a church meeting with a guy who was so suspicious that I was going to run off that he made me wear bright green flip-flops on my feet so that I couldn't run away – and it was the middle of winter!

At the meeting I spoke with someone who could relate to me because he had a similar background to me. After our conversation I simply said to God, 'if you are real then I give you my life and all the mess I am in, please help me sort it out'. Someone then asked if they could pray with me and ask God to help me with my drug addiction. I thought 'whatever!' I reckoned I'd nothing to lose and everything to gain if this God was able to help, so I agreed. To my amazement, after this guy had stopped praying, the painful withdrawal symptoms of my addiction stopped! I didn't go through a detox programme or take any medicines yet I didn't suffer the usual pains of heroin withdrawal. From that point on I have never taken heroin and that was nearly six years ago.

As a consequence of the way I had lived, my whole life needed rebuilding. So I started a rehabilitation programme run by a Christian organisation called Teen Challenge. There I began to develop a sense of responsibility and a value for myself. After completing the programme I worked there as a staff member and step by step I began to rebuild my life again. Whilst working there I went to India and Africa for a few months at a time to do building work on orphanages and rehab centres. For the first time in my life I was actually doing something that benefited others and not myself!

I came back to the Abundant Life Church, Bradford nearly three years ago, a completely different person. I had rebuilt relationships within my family circle and I was finally a son whom my Mum could be proud of. I began work and I went back to college to further my construction skills. I am now at the early stages of developing my own construction business and have bought a great house.

Despite many years apart I began to rebuild my relationship with my daughter Collette – I started to embrace the responsibilities of being a Dad and we have really built up something very special. I love her to bits; she is my little princess!

And to top it all off, in God's House I met a beautiful lady called Donna who has completely captured my heart. With her I now know what true love is and I am head over heals in love with her. We are at the beginnings of building a fantastic life together.

It amazes me as I compare where I was in life without God to where I am now. Only a few years ago I could have been a name in an obituary column. Not only has God restored my life, he has taken me beyond restoration to a life that is prospering in all areas. As I have remained planted in God's House, I have flourished as a person in my soul and character where honesty and integrity are now the foundations of my life. I have a life where my dreams have become a reality, it is a life beyond my wildest dreams and I can walk with dignity with my head held high.

If I can do it, so can you!

Tim Haigh

MITCH
FLYING HIGH

"GOD'S HOUSE IS A GREENHOUSE OF GROWTH
WHERE DESTINIES ARE EXPLODING INTO BLOOM
AND DREAMS ARE BEING REALISED"

THE FUTURE
FLOURISHING

CHAPTER 5

FLOURISHING IN THE HOUSE

'*The righteous will flourish like a palm tree. They will grow like a cedar of Lebanon. Planted in the house of the Lord they will flourish in the courts of our God. They will still bear fruit in old age, they will stay fresh and green'*[1]

A sure sign that you're planted in God's House, is that everything around you is flourishing. God's House is a greenhouse of growth, where destinies are exploding into bloom and dreams are being realised. In this environment, you will flourish.

Flourishing is not only about the atmosphere of a church but also about the hearts of the people there. The scripture above shows a clear link between being planted in the House and flourishing and, as they say, 'home is where the heart is'. Therefore, flourishing is a choice, a choice about where you put your heart. Many people who attend church are in God's House but they've not made the decision to put their heart, life and soul there. To them it's just one house among many, not their spiritual home.

You need to make God's House your home, because once you commit to being in the House it brings a depth to your world and consistency to your life. Consistency is an important ingredient missing from many churches today. But in the scripture we read the language of consistency; we are to be 'planted' and 'rooted'. In other words, consumed. It means being in one place long enough to call it home. Too many people in God's House are inconsistent and for them, church is a game of hokey-kokey. They are in, out, in, out, and more often than not, shaking their commitment all about! But until they put their roots down and become planted, they will never maximise their ability to flourish.

A while ago we had our good friends John and Lara over for dinner. I decided to make lasagne, a simple dish for someone like me who has limited culinary skills. When it came to serving up the dinner, the lasagne looked more like soup than pasta. Its consistency was all wrong. It was so runny we had to eat it with a spoon! I couldn't understand where I had gone wrong until at 3.00am the next morning, when I sat bolt upright in bed as the realisation of what I had done dawned on me: 'I forgot to put the lasagne sheets in it!' I shrieked in the darkness waking my poor husband up. There was a missing ingredient which had made the consistency of my lasagne all wrong! And over the years I have come to the conclusion that too many Christians are missing their lasagne sheets. They go from church to church uprooting and planting, uprooting and planting and then wonder why things in their lives just aren't flourishing. But planting takes time and just as in the natural realm a bud will not blossom after just one week in the soil, neither will it in the spiritual. They must give up their consumer mentality towards God's House and put down some roots.

Despite the benefits of staying planted in the House, some Christians continue to uproot themselves and keep moving around. They join your church and make a big entrance as they walk through the front door announcing that they are here for the long haul. But as soon as they don't like the way you are running the House, or they aren't happy with your choice of furnishings, they begin to pack their suitcase and make their way towards the back door. Consumers think that God's House has a revolving door; one which they can go in and out of at will. The sad truth for these people is that they will never enjoy the benefits which only come from being in the same place long term. Their experience of church will always be shallow like their roots.

LIVING STONES OR MOVING BRICKS?

It is difficult to build anything magnificent with moving bricks. That's why many church leaders are frustrated and tired of people who say they are called to be part of the House, but refuse to settle down and play their part in building it long-term. They are moving bricks, people who never stay in one place long enough to build anything of value. Peter describes each individual Christian as a *'living stone'* [2] and the Amplified Bible puts it this way: *'Come and like living stones be yourselves built into a spiritual house.'* It's our job to come and be built into God's House as a living stone not a moving brick.

A living stone gets built into the structure of God's House and contributes its life, strength and support to the whole building. It can carry weight, as it becomes part of the framework of the house. You can get a lot done with living stones but moving bricks are a disaster waiting to happen.

A moving brick in the House of God violates the very purpose it was created for. No builder wants to build with moving bricks; they weaken the building and make it an unsafe place for others to enter. All that's placed on them, all the responsibility, all the people and the trust invested in them, collapses as these bricks move on. And, every other brick built alongside it is damaged in the process. Consequently, leaders end up spending many hours repairing broken walls and collapsing ministries because they went ahead and built on what they thought was a living stone, but it was actually a moving brick.

I built myself into the House of God many years ago and despite the many opportunities and offers presented to me and my husband, we have refused to budge. I don't want to live my life moving from one building site to another. I want to stay in one place long enough to build a House which is large, magnificent and worthy of God's name. And in doing this, God has brought the most amazing opportunities to my life. You don't have to go chasing opportunities because if you are faithful, God will bring every opportunity, relationship, provision and resource you will ever need into your world.

Jesus said, *'Remain in me and I will remain in you. No branch can bear fruit by itself. It must remain in the vine.'*[3] If you want to bear much fruit, you have got to remain. I have seen amazing examples of God's favour on people who are planted in the House. These people, having given their heart to the House, are now flourishing in every area of their lives. They are being promoted at work, their businesses are growing and they are prospering in every area. They were advised to move and chase that job opportunity or relationship by the consumers in their world, but their refusal to go has resulted in much fruit coming from their lives.

CHECK YOUR SOIL

Sometimes, those who are desperate to flourish face an agonising problem as the place they originally chose to be planted in, has now become a place where they are unable to flourish. This happens because our opening scripture in this chapter has two parts to the equation. Many pastors and leaders have preached from this verse and emphasised to all in the House that they must 'settle down and be committed.' While this is true, my prayer is that every pastor has also made the same commitment to keep the soil that those plants are being encouraged to sink their roots deeply into, productive and healthy. It is the job of leaders to fertilize and maintain great soil so that every plant can flourish.

It brings me great sadness to see good people having to uproot and leave a church where they've served faithfully year after year. They have been completely committed, they have loved the Pastor and they have tried with all their heart to get planted in that House. But for all their planting, five or ten years on they are still not flourishing. They are good people who have a great attitude and a desire to serve God. But their kids aren't flourishing, their marriage isn't flourishing and their life is not moving to the next level. The soil in that House is in poor condition. In the natural, perfectly strong, healthy plants cannot thrive if they are placed in bad soil and the same is true for people spiritually. We need soil that is rich in nutrients; it needs to nurture the potential in people and grow them into all they have the potential to be.

Just as every heart has a soil condition, like Jesus taught in the parable of the four soils, so does the heart of every church.[4] Don't let the soil of your House become overcrowded, don't let it become full of unnecessary pollutants, and don't let the plants become choked by out of control weeds in the soil of your House. Every good builder of God's House has committed to tilling the soil and feeding it with the rich nutrients of Gods word. It must be watered regularly with his presence and frequently raked over to remove pestilence of any kind. Our soil needs to be like the good soil Jesus spoke of: *'But the seed that falls on good soil stands for those with a noble and good heart who, when they hear the word, retain it and by persevering in it produce a crop'*[5]. In other words, good soil plus good seed equals a harvest.

POT BOUND

I am not a great gardener; in fact I am not a gardener at all. I once planted some bulbs and eagerly awaited their arrival in the spring. I waited, and kept on waiting but they never appeared. Frustrated, I eventually asked my Mum why they had not appeared. She dug up what I had planted and informed me that I had planted them upside down! I didn't know such a thing was possible. But then if it was, I guess my flowers would be blooming in some garden in Australia! Anyway, despite my failed efforts, I do know that growing plants need re-potting from time to time. The pot in which I plant my new seeds, and in which it grows its first green shoots, will soon not be big enough to permit the development of the flowers that are waiting to flourish within that plant. It will have to be re-potted into a larger vessel.

It's the responsibility of the leaders in God's House to ensure that people's lives do not become pot bound. Make sure there is space in your soil for people to bud and blossom all the year round. Give people room to grow, space to put down strong root systems. I wonder? If the youth ministry in your House flourished more than your personal ministry, would that be OK? Would there be enough room in your pot for both of you? Many church splits have taken place for no other reason than the pot was too small for both ministries to grow in.

Our challenge is to build a House where there is room for everyone to flourish. A House in which we can stand back and be amazed as each small seed becomes a strong shoot, a firm young plant, a mature shrub and eventually becomes a blossoming tree that produces delicious fruit which people from around the world will come to eat.

[1] Psalm 92:12-14
[2] 1 Peter 2:5
[3] John 15:4
[4] Luke 8:4
[5] Luke 8:15

"IT'S THE RESPONSIBILITY OF THE LEADERS
TO ENSURE THAT PEOPLE HAVE ROOM TO FLOURISH"

'My life was once in tatters but is now thriving in the fertile soil of God's House.'

In June 1993, aged 25, I walked into God's House with my life in complete tatters.

I was homeless, depressed, suicidal and addicted to amphetamines. I had no mates, my girlfriend had left me, I had no job, no prospects and certainly no future. My dignity had been stripped away by a life of drug and alcohol fuelled violence and deceit. Since my late teens I had been heavily involved in organised football violence, travelling the country every week to take part in gang fights with rival clubs. I had earned a fearsome reputation as a notorious football hooligan and local criminal. My crimes were committed all over the country and caused me to be constantly on the run from the Police. I was eventually arrested and charged. In the process I ruined the lives of my parents, from whom I stole money and possessions from their home, and the lives of everyone I had dragged into my circle of crime. I was a completely dysfunctional person who was on a path to self-destruction.

One night in desperation I went to church and reached out to a God who I had left behind many years earlier. I realised he had never left me but still loved me and wanted to forgive me for everything I had done. I gave my life to Jesus that very moment and made a commitment to love him and walk with him for the rest of my life. I have never looked back.

As I left the church that night, I remember feeling a mixture of gratitude for the life God had handed me back, a fear of hurting people again, and uncertainty about what the future would hold. I continued to walk with God and my life began to change.

A while later I met my wife Esther who was also a Christian. She had a daughter called Annie and I was amazed that God not only gave me a beautiful wife but also trusted me with the life of a child! We grew as a family and now have three more gorgeous children. Over the next few years God slowly helped me put my life back together and as a family we began to discover his plan for our future together.

We served God and became active members of the church where I had spent my early years. Over a period of time, it became evident that there was little room to grow and I began to understand why I had left God's House disillusioned and disinterested all those years ago. I realised that my kids would end up going the same way if we stayed there.

We felt a real yearning to grow; yet we weren't changing and began to question why we felt like this. I was walking strong with God on a personal level and was working for the church as a youth worker but something was still missing. That year I handed my notice in and prepared for the next move. We were ready to do whatever it would take to make sure we were in the right environment to grow.

After months of searching through job vacancies and training programs we watched an interview with Paul Scanlon on the God Channel. As we listened to him talk Esther and I felt like all the confusion and 'missing' stuff from our lives was slowly being unravelled. Shortly after this I was given a copy of the 'Voice to the Nations' magazine and saw an advert for the Abundant Life Leadership Academy.

I joined the course and nine months later graduated as Student of the Year. It was the first time I had successfully completed anything in my life. By the time the course had finished we had relocated to Bradford so we could be planted in this House.

In the last two years we have all grown more than in the previous seven. Its great to see our kids planted and flourishing, knowing they are being equipped to make great choices in life. I now work for the church heading up the Community Action Teams which reach out into the inner city areas and Esther has also completed the Leadership Academy.

We have become increasingly aware of how being planted in God's House really does enable you to flourish, as individuals and as a family. Our relationship with each other and with our children has got even stronger and we have a more positive attitude towards life. We now make better, wiser choices and have a greater understanding of how to live out our walk with God in a non-religious, incredibly fun way but without compromise!

Life is never perfect and we do go through difficult times just like everyone else. But being planted in God's House means we are now stronger and better equipped to deal with them.

My life was once in tatters but is now thriving in the fertile soil of God's House.

Matt Stockdale

COMMUNITY ACTION
TEAMS

"WE ARE TO PREPARE THE WAY FOR A HURTING WORLD
TO FIND A HOUSE
WHICH THEY CAN MAKE THEIR HOME"

FINDING A NEED AND FILLING IT

CHAPTER 6

PREPARATION

E very opportunity I have had in life, first presented itself as hard work. Building God's House means a lifetime of hard work. I'm sorry if this comes as bad news to you but it doesn't get any less demanding over time. Building the House is like raising a growing family. The more kids you have the more needs are generated. You have to extend your house, buy more furniture, feed more mouths and pay more bills. A growing House is always full of opportunities but they look a lot like hard work.

People in our church often joke that they dare not go on holiday in case they miss something because the House is changing and being built so fast – all a result of hard work. Some have even had the tapes from the meeting sent to their holiday address. Now that is consumed! So, if you have come to God's House for the glamour or chance to show off your interior design abilities then please read on because without a good work ethic, nothing gets done. And building a great House for God means we all have to learn to love preparation.

Preparation is the part of the building process that everyone wants to bypass. No one volunteers to strip the wall, sand the floorboards or peel off the paint. But everyone wants to help put the nice ornaments out. Preparation is long, tiring and for the most part unseen. It is hard work. This book has taken years of preparation. It contains some of the lessons I have learned in my efforts to build this House. But for you it's a few hours of reading in a comfortable chair with a warm cup of coffee. If you want to build something then you have to make preparation part of your life. This House needs consumed people who will not close their eyes to the peeling plaster but will roll their sleeves up and get stuck in.

Preparation is so important to God that when he was about to send his only son into the world, he made a plan to first prepare the way. He wanted someone to go ahead of his son and make sure that some foundations had been established. There were some paths to be smoothed out to ensure that Jesus arrived in a prepared world, a world ready to hear the good news. John the Baptist was the one sent to prepare the way for Jesus. And I believe that like John, every consumed life is also called to prepare the way for the gospel to impact their community. We are to prepare the way for a hurting world to find a House which they can make their home.

The Message translation gives us an insight into the job description of a 'preparer of the way'. Speaking about John it states, *'He went all through the country around the Jordan River preaching a baptism of life changing, leading to forgiveness of sins as described in the words of Isaiah the prophet. 'Thunder in the desert, prepare God's arrival! Make the road smooth and straight! Every ditch will be filled in, every bump smoothed out, the detours straightened out, all the ruts paved over.'* [1] If Jesus needed someone to prepare the way for him 2000 years ago then he still needs a people to prepare a way for his message today.

John spent his entire life smoothing out the bumps, filling in the ditches and paving over ruts. When you commit to building God's House you too will also spend a lot of time smoothing out the bumps in people's lives, filling out the ditches in people's understanding and paving over the ruts so that the House is fully prepared for everyone who will dwell there. We may think preparation is insignificant but when Jesus was asked who the greatest prophet was he said, *'I tell you the truth among those born of women there has not risen anyone greater than John the Baptist.'* [2] If you were asked the same question, someone like Elijah might come to mind because he called down fire from heaven and could outrun a chariot. That seems far more exciting. But to Jesus the greatest wasn't the person who had performed the best but the one who had prepared the best. It takes a special kind of person to give their life to the cause of his House, to work for hours in the basement just digging a strong foundation. John was not after popularity he just wanted to prepare the way for Jesus. We must have the same attitude if we are to stay content, consumed and fulfilled in building God's House.

PREPARATION REMOVES THE ROT

Let me share with you a few things I have learnt about preparation. Preparation is definitely not glamorous. If you can find me a glamorous builder then they are probably not building anything significant. Builders are easy to spot in a crowd. From their bruised and rough hands to their badly dented nails, to the scars on their arms from where they have been carrying heavy loads of bricks, to their worn out trouser legs from kneeling in the dirt. Builders have a certain look which tells you a lot about what they have been doing all day. The same is true in God's House. You can easily tell who the serious builders are and who the people are that just like to talk about building. If you want to be consumed by the House you need to learn to live with broken nails and dirty hands.

Building God's House involves dealing with the rot that has long overstayed its welcome. It involves stripping back the old layers of tradition, religion, and exclusiveness that have decorated the walls of the church for years. Believe me, you cannot handle this stuff without getting messy.

In our last house all the windows had become rotten and needed replacing. But we were too busy to deal with the problem properly so we just kept putting new layers of paint over the rotting wood. That was fine until I became pregnant and wanted to use the room with the worst window as a nursery. Another layer of paint was no longer good enough because we had a precious baby on the way who deserved better. We now had a new incentive to deal with the rot. We had to commit to preparing the room properly so it was time to sand down the window, remove the frame and get a new one fitted. When the preparations were in place to put the new window in God spoke to me about his House saying, 'Charlotte, when my House is prepared to deal with the rot, then I will be able to send new spiritual babies to it. But I will not let the new cohabit with the old rot.'

God wants to bless your House with new friendships, opportunities and resources but he won't send these to a House where they will be made to share a room with the rot of gossip, or the rot of control and traditionalism. It is far easier to ignore and paint over that rotten deacon, who is gossiping about the House and undermining the pastor than deal with it. But the truth is until we deal with it, your new house-guests cannot arrive.

Preparation ensures that a strong foundation is laid. It involves digging down deep and is the training ground for all you have in your heart to build. Every success we have comes because of the preparation we put in and we must never try to bypass the process. You may want to launch new ministries or conferences but unless you prepare for them properly, you won't be able to overcome the challenges that the new initiatives bring with them. Many times people have come to our House and decided to try and copy one of the ministries that has particularly inspired them. They visited a prison and now want a prison ministry, they saw our buses bringing in hundreds of needy families and are now on the phone trying to buy a second hand vehicle. But before any of those ministries were established, we had to spend a lot of time preparing the way. Make friends with preparation and enjoy it because the lessons you learn on your journey will become some of the treasures that eventually adorn the walls of the house you are building.

PREPARATION IS A WELCOME MAT

Have you ever visited someone's home to discover they weren't prepared for you? A few years ago I was visiting some of my husband's family in the USA. His Granny Ethel lived some distance away from the rest of the family in Washington State, so we arranged to make the long drive and go have dinner with her. Ethel was a sweetheart and very old. I remember seeing the look of shock on her face as she saw us at her front door. She was embarrassed because she had forgotten we were coming and was unprepared for our arrival. She then spent the whole time apologising for her house not being clean and for her hair not being washed. That feeling of awkwardness we had because Granny wasn't expecting us is the same feeling people get when they arrive at a church that hasn't prepared for them.

When I became pregnant, people could tell I was expecting a baby long before there were any obvious signs of the pregnancy in my physical body. They could tell by looking at the books I was reading, my endless magazines on parenting and the new baby clothes that were beginning to fill my closet. In the same way, preparation tells the world what you are expecting before it arrives. And you can't embrace into your world something you are unprepared for. Before we crossed our church over we had to spend months preparing the way for the new people we wanted to embrace. We had to deal with the rot of prejudice, traditionalism and control in the House and throw out the peeling wallpaper of intolerance. It was hard work and costly but it changed our House forever. We could then welcome all kinds of people into our house who previously wouldn't have dreamed of coming because there was no welcome mat for their arrival. Every person who has entered our House since then has no idea of the lengths our leadership team went to in preparing the way for them. They just feel at home and soon find themselves being consumed with zeal for the House that embraced them and gave them the opportunity for a fresh start.

PREPARATION IS A LEGACY

Preparation is an important legacy to leave for those who will take over the running of the House when your time comes to an end. When I look at King David's life I see a great example of one generation passing on their zeal for the House to the next. He was passionate about God's House and loved everything about it. His dream was to rebuild the temple in Jerusalem and if he hadn't given in to the temptation of Bathsheba, he may well have achieved it. When God told David that Solomon would build his House, David did not become bitter or resign, neither did he go home and sulk. Instead David devoted his life to preparing the way for this to happen. He fought many battles and defeated enemies to ensure that Solomon's reign would be a time of peace, one in which he could concentrate on building God's House. King David spent his life gathering treasure and provisions for the House his son would build. He put in much of the hard work in advance, so that someone else could complete the work. Eventually he handed the responsibility of building the temple over to Solomon saying, *'My son Solomon is young and inexperienced and the house to be built for the Lord should be of great magnificence and fame and splendor in the sight of all the nations. Therefore I will make preparations for it. David made extensive preparations before his death, then he called his son Solomon and charged him to build a house for the Lord.'* [3]

David handed on to the next generation the tools and resources they needed to get the job done. This is a great picture of how our work to build a magnificent House for God should continue from one generation to another. I have watched my own father making extensive preparations, dealing with battles and winning fights, simply to prepare the way for the next generation. I have watched as he has led our team out into battle and observed just how ruthless he has been in preparing a way from the foundations up. The House of God should always be a place where there is a seamless transition from one generation to the next.

We must build the House with our future church in mind, not only with what we have right now. When we built a 2000 seat auditorium for a church of about 400 people, some thought we were mad. But we could see the future clearly and carried in our hearts the thousands of people who would come to dwell in our House. We prepared for them in advance and ensured that there was plenty of room for all the new ministries, initiatives, resources and people that were coming to the House. Now, with over 2000 people coming through the doors each week, we are preparing for the next stage of building the House. Why? Because we want to hand future generations some awesome facilities and resources, rather than sending them back to the beginning again.

PREPARATION IS CONTINUOUS

Finally, we need to realise that the work of preparation never ends because once we have dealt with the rotting window, we find a burst pipe, followed by a blown fuse, and so the list goes on.

When we moved into our new house, all ready to settle down, we were asked by the foreman to go round and complete a snag list. We had to look for any problems that had appeared since the house had been built. We found leaking taps, cracked tiles and a sink that was installed at an angle far from the horizontal! Just when we thought we could settle down, another list of things appeared. And so it is with God's House. This is why we must live lives that are consumed with zeal, because at times our flat out zeal for the House is the only thing that keeps us going. We press on simply because we love God's House and refuse to compromise on the way we build it.

Don't settle for second best. Don't build God a bungalow when he asked you to build a House. Be true to your calling and the blueprint for God's House he has given you. And develop a heart like John the Baptist who gave himself thoroughly to being a 'preparer of the way'.

[1] Luke 3:3
[2] Matthew 11:11
[3] 1 Chronicles 22:14-19

THE HOUSE OF GOD SHOULD ALWAYS BE A PLACE
WHERE THERE IS A SEAMLESS TRANSITION
FROM ONE GENERATION TO THE NEXT

THREE GENERATIONS

DANNY & HEATHER'S STORY

'This House believes in empowering the next generation.'

We are only young but we have a thriving business, which is in no small part due to us being firmly planted in God's House. Here's our story… so far!

Heather grew up in God's House; she's been part of the Abundant Life Church since she was born! I got saved when I was 16, after being introduced to church by Heather who was on the same fashion course at college. After a couple of months we started dating and helped by the teaching of the church we conducted a good relationship. We studied fashion for two years and toward the end of our second year both applied to the top universities in the world because we are taught to aim high.

However, we soon found that God had a different plan for our lives. What society thinks we should do is not always what God wants us to do and for us that was the case. We came to understand that God wanted us to have the desires of our heart but that we should go down another route in order to get closer to achieving it. So, we turned down the offers we had to attend one of the top colleges in the fashion world, which in the eyes of some was committing long-term career suicide. Anyway, we knew God was in control and if he didn't want us at university then he had something better in store for us - and he did!

We both hold one message that was preached at church particularly close to our hearts. It helped inspire everything we did from then on. The message was about how God doesn't do all the work for us, instead he wants us to do the groundwork, which he'll honour, and then work with us from that point on, one step at a time. For us it meant stepping out in faith, putting our groundwork in and trusting God for the rest.

The dream we had was to start our own fashion design company. And as soon as we made the decision to turn down the university placements and do it, God confirmed we had made the right decision. At church one Sunday morning, just before worship, our pastor blessed us with an envelope containing a £500 cheque with which to start our business. That morning he practically demonstrated what he preaches, that this House believes in empowering the next generation.

Every thing we learned in God's House, we applied to our business. At first things were hard and we felt we weren't getting anywhere but we had no doubt in our minds we were doing the right thing and kept on persevering. We were clear about where God wanted to take us and how he wanted to use us in the fashion world. Our dream was to be the most successful young designers in the world, and through that to be able to reach out to people in that circle of life.

In December 2001 we got engaged which was brilliant, but it also marked the most faith-testing time of our lives so far. The wedding was set for the following August and the business wasn't bringing in enough money so we both got part time jobs in telesales. This didn't discourage us at all, God wanted the best for us, we just needed to do our bit. In this period the business took more of a back seat but we knew it was only for a short period while we were saving and planning for the wedding. Mixing our faith with common sense, over the next eight months we managed to pay for an expensive wedding and had some money to spare. Our bank balance kept telling us we couldn't afford it, but we refused to accept that God wanted to give us less than we were believing for, and he was faithful. We didn't hold back on any extras on the wedding day. It was such a good feeling on the day to look around and see what faith can achieve. We knew that getting married was the next step up in our lives and in the business.

On our actual wedding day, which of course took place in God's House, Danny was offered a job working for another fashion business being run by a couple in the church, which was thriving. This was brilliant because we had just taken another risk by quitting our part time jobs.

We got back from honeymoon exited about what God was going to throw at us next. Danny started his job designing suits and not long after Heather was also given a job. The owners of the company really believed in us and knew our dream. After a month working there, Danny was introduced to a footballer through the owner and showed him the range of T-shirts we had been putting together. The client loved them and ordered ten! Within a few months we had both resigned our positions and were able to run our own business full-time. Before too long we had over twenty premiership footballers as clients. We did this with total backing and encouragement from our old employers who truly believed in our ability.

It seemed like almost overnight our profile in the fashion world had risen to such a high level that on a daily basis we were getting phone calls from major celebrities asking us to design for them. At first it was a bit overwhelming but at the same time we knew this is what God had planned for us.

We had always known what we wanted to do and believed we'd get there one day. We just didn't realise it would come so fast! It just goes to show that if you are planted in God's House, you will flourish. It's now been eighteen months since things really took off and our business continues to thrive. Almost every major name in football is wearing our clothes. We have built up some great friendships with our clients and we get to share about our beliefs and our faith, which at the end of the day is what we're supposed to do. Things have happened so fast, but we know this is how God wants it to be if we are to achieve our dream of being the youngest, most successful fashion designers known to people. We have still got a long way to go but realise that if we keep active and rooted in God's House, there is no limit to where we can go and who we can reach.

Finally, we want to say a big 'thank you' to every one who has believed in us. If it wasn't for your encouragement we wouldn't be the people we are today and we certainly wouldn't have the success we've achieved. We especially want to thank the leaders at church and the youth team for telling us we can do it. And to that special couple who gave us the start to an amazing business journey, THANK YOU.

Danny + Heather

Danny & Heather Greig

OUR
ANNUAL CHRISTMAS GIVEAWAY
HUNDREDS OF GIFTS GIVEN TO THE
CHILDREN OF OUR CITY

"THE HOUSE OF GOD SHOULD NEVER BE CAUGHT SHORT
IT SHOULD BE A PLACE OF STOCKPILES OF PROVISION
TO BLESS OTHERS WITH"

GOODIE BAGS AWAITING CHERISH DELEGATES

CHAPTER 7

IS ABIGAIL
IN THE HOUSE?

Let's begin this chapter with a story. This is a story of three people, David, Nabal and Abigail.[1] Nabal was a very wealthy man. He had one thousand goats and three thousand sheep which, by today's standards, means he was loaded! He had more than a few fleeces to spare. It was shearing time at Nabal's house in Carmel, a time associated with festivity and rejoicing.

Meanwhile, same time different scene, we find David. He is tired from battle and the pursuit of Saul, and is camping out with his men in the nearby desert. Hungry and in need of refreshment, he had heard that Nabal was having a party celebrating harvest time. So, David sent his men to see Nabal with the following message:

'Long life to you, good health to you and your household and good health to all that is yours. Now I hear that it is sheep shearing time. When your shepherds were with us we did not mistreat them and the whole time they were at Carmel nothing of theirs was missing...

Therefore be favourable towards my young men since we have come at a festive time.'

Nabal's response was not what David expected. Because it came from someone who obviously had more than enough, he was surprised to be told, *'Why should I take my bread and water, the meat that I have slaughtered for my shearers and give it to men coming from who knows where?'*

Nabal had much but wanted to keep it all for himself. You would think that if he had three thousand sheep he could spare a few. He had been blessed with an abundance, and here was an opportunity to share it with others, but he chose to turn down this opportunity and instead hurled insults at David's men. He sent David's men away with nothing. David's men went to a place of fullness and came away empty handed. How sad.

Did you know that churches can also be like this? People like David will approach a church because they are attracted by the sounds coming from the House, the sounds of singing, joy and celebration for all that God has done. But they can leave that same House with nothing more than they entered with. In fact, if they put the little they had into the offering, they may even leave with less than they came in with! Churches like this are churches full of fat sheep who are all hanging on to their fleeces and unwilling to share their blessings.

We're in a world where people are searching. People are in need of warmth, of friendship and of hope. Meanwhile, too many fat sheep are sitting in churches feeding their faces when they should be letting go of their fleeces and offering them to people in the world. It's time for them to give their lives away but many of them run off bucking and bolting at the sight of a pair of shears! Fat sheep have a consumer mentality. The House of God becomes all about their needs and their comfort.

AN ABIGAIL SPIRIT

When the servants in Nabal's household saw the way he refused to help David, they knew there was going to be trouble. So they went to find Nabal's wife, Abigail.

Abigail was a beautiful, intelligent woman who had a reputation for getting things done. When she heard what had happened she wasted no time and left everything she was doing to ensure this situation got sorted out quickly:

'Abigail lost no time. She took two hundred loaves of bread, two skins of wine, five dressed sheep, five seahs of roasted grain, a hundred cakes of raisins and two hundred cakes of pressed figs and loaded them on donkeys.'

Abigail was a resourceful woman; she had extra supplies just waiting to bless people with. Where else would you get two hundred loaves of bread? Do you have them in your cupboard at home?

The House of God should never be caught short. It should be a place with stockpiles of provision for the sole purpose of meeting the needs of others. There should be stockpiles of peace, not a fragile peace that will only stretch to those already in the House. There should be stockpiles of acceptance ready to be given away. It was as if Abigail knew a demand would be made of her and she was prepared. The House of God needs to be like that. It should be a place of abundance where we are never caught lacking. Whether it is love, peace, friendship or acceptance that people need, we should always have enough to give away. Abigail is a picture of how our churches must be. Abigail means 'the joy of her Father' and when churches have a spirit like hers, they are truly the joy of their heavenly Father.

By way of contrast, Nabal was foolish by both name and nature. His name actually means 'foolish'. Don't be foolish like Nabal and turn away people who need help when they come knocking at your door. He was so comfortable with life that he had forgotten what it was like to be in need. However much God blesses you with, never forget what it was like the day you first came to Christ, empty and searching. Never forget how the lost feel or lose touch with the power of sharing your blessing with those less fortunate than you. Never let God's House become the house of a fool!

David's men were a highly armed and trained fighting unit. They were not the sort of guys to pick a fight with but Nabal's selfishness put him and his entire household in danger. The same is true for every House of God. One person's selfishness, one leader's withholding, or one refusal to fill a need should be a warning sign to all who dwell in that House. The alarm bells should start to ring and all those who are consumed with zeal for the House should start to cry out. We have a motto in our church, it is 'Find a need and fill it'. Nabal would not support this kind of emphasis. So, stop waiting around for the Nabals in your world to grant you permission to help the Davids who enter your world. Nabal can represent any House that, even though richly blessed by God, has ceased to be a storehouse for the world they are sent to reach. Instead, they are acting like a larder, stockpiled with provision for their own benefit. The House that we are called to build must have an Abigail spirit.

Abigail did not want others to suffer because of Nabal's foolishness and she was willing to put her own life at risk for the sake of her household. She feared God more than she feared man, and when you are consumed like that you do whatever it takes.

There will always be people like Nabal in the House of God. And as you are reading this faces are probably springing to mind. However, the challenge we face is to find the same courage as Abigail did to bypass the 'fools' and go and help the hungry Davids in our world. We need to be churches of sheared sheep. We need to give away our fleeces. I hope you don't arrive at church each week to get your fleece combed but go ready to be sheared. Shear your financial seed, shear your friendship, shear your kindness. Just think: if we all let go of our fleeces, there would be no one in our world that would have to stay in the cold any longer.

Just imagine for a minute that you are David. You tried to gain favour from the household of Nabal but found the cupboard to be bare. Then suddenly your hope is restored as a small, frail figure on a donkey loaded with fig cakes begins to head your way. David, who was ready to go and fight Nabal, was now disarmed by Abigail and her 'bakewell tart'.

We have learned how to disarm people in our city with the equivalent of Abigail's bakewell tart. In our church we have teams that visit people living on some of the most deprived housing estates in our city. Our teams go and introduce themselves by simply asking, 'is there anything we can do for you'. There is no preaching, there is no demand to attend a service, they don't even try to get them to say the 'prayer of salvation' on the doorstep. The aim is simply to love and serve people. That may seem far too insignificant a task for some people to spend their time doing. But so many times that seemingly insignificant act has literally saved a life as someone from our team has called at the house just as someone was about to do something very damaging or even kill themselves.

Abigail's seemingly insignificant act of taking her cakes and figs to David resulted in her capturing the heart of the future king. David found Abigail irresistible and the world will find churches with the spirit of Abigail irresistible too.

Abigail won David's heart with her wisdom, her resourcefulness, her grace and her beauty. In an amazing turn of events involving the death of Nabal, Abigail went from being the wife of a fool to marrying the future king. God is looking for a church worthy of marriage to the King. Jesus is not coming back for a dysfunctional House he is coming back for a beautiful bride. A House that is irresistible to the world.

Does your House have the Abigail spirit?

[1] 1 Samuel 25

"JESUS IS NOT COMING BACK FOR A DYSFUNCTIONAL HOUSE
HE IS COMING BACK FOR A BEAUTIFUL BRIDE"

'Simon has been out of rehab
for over a year now and has got himself
plugged into church by serving in any area
he was needed. Today he is in charge of all the
cooking and feeding of the homeless done
by the church's Community Action Teams -
it is just amazing!'

I grew up in a Christian family and went to church every week but as a teenager found it boring and irrelevant. When I was 16, I met a boy and stopped going to church altogether. I ended up pregnant and went on to marry him. By the time I was 19 we had two children. Three years on, things started to go drastically wrong. He couldn't handle the responsibilities of having a wife and two children and started drinking heavily. He would be out drinking 'till all hours; he drank all the money we had and me and the kids were left with nothing. This went on for the best part of a year until one day I tried talking to him but he got angry and took his frustrations out on me. On it went and I became trapped by the fear of his violence.

It suddenly hit me that I didn't have to live in this fear all the time. That's when I heard God say to me, 'I am still here, I never left you, you left me'. As a result I plucked up the courage to leave my husband and moved back to Yorkshire with my two girls for a totally fresh start.

By this time I had recommitted my life to Christ. It was about two years later that I met Simon. He gave his life to Christ at my church and started to face up to some of his problems. Simon had been heavily into taking drugs for the last fourteen years, and I knew this when I met him but God told me to trust him and so I did. Within a year of meeting we were married.

For the first year or so of our marriage Simon struggled with his addiction. The church we attended weren't equipped to deal with him so he was not growing in his faith or changing in his life-style. He was using heavily, spending much of our money on his habit and stealing from me as well. Our relationship was under incredible pressure.

Around that time we heard about this church in Bradford through some friends of my parents, so we decided to go and visit out of curiosity. The minute we walked in we knew it was where we were meant to be; it was home. We started to travel over as much as we could but we had no transport of our own. We did this for about a year. Desperate for the positive change that we sensed was linked to us getting plugged into God's House in Bradford, we took the plunge and moved to the city simply to get involved in the Abundant Life Church.

This step of faith resulted in us being put in touch with people who could help Simon. He was referred to a Christian rehabilitation centre and went into detox. While he was away I took the opportunity of getting more involved in God's House. I started to serve at the homeless breakfasts each Friday as well as helping in the Family Centre on Wednesdays. Now, eighteen months on, I am employed by the Family Centre as a support worker.

Simon has been out of rehab for over a year now and has got himself plugged into church by serving in any area he was needed. Today he is in charge of all the cooking and feeding of the homeless done by the church's Community Action Teams - it is just amazing! He has been clean for so long we have now stopped counting how long it is since he last took drugs. We are looking forwards not backwards; we have a hope and a future as a family. Simon plans to join the church's Leadership Academy next year and we just know that God will take us from strength to strength.

Being planted in God's House, we have truly flourished. Our girls, Charlotte and Amy are now settled and happy. Before they were badly affected by the mess we had created, and Charlotte was really struggling at school, but now she is doing really well. Our lives have never been the same since we made the decision to get ourselves planted in God's House and invest our lives into its mission. We have realized that it doesn't matter how much you do or what you do, if you aren't planted in the House serving God, you will never receive all that God has for you.

Simon & Ruth

Ruth & Simon Emery

"OUR HOUSE IS EXCELLENT IN APPEARANCE
BUT IS NOT A MUSEUM
IT IS A WORK PLACE"

BUILT TO BE ENJOYED

CHAPTER 8

YOUR HOUSE IS A GIFT

J esus lived everyday of his life, not as a giver but as a gift. He was a gift to everyone he came into contact with. Scripture tells us that, *'God so loved the world that he gave his only son.'* [1] He didn't just send, lend or share him; he gave him as a gift.

Consider for a moment what Jesus actually gave. He gave:

❖ Honour to his parents
❖ Respect to his teachers
❖ Wisdom to his disciples
❖ Patience to Thomas
❖ A second chance to Peter
❖ Forgiveness to his executioners
❖ Inclusion to Zacchaeus
❖ Healing to the cripple
❖ Dignity to the prostitute
❖ Wine to the newlyweds
❖ A knee for children to sit on
❖ Tears of compassion to Mary and Martha

Jesus gave the 'kiss of life' to everyone he encountered, he was the ultimate gift of life. Notice that Jesus didn't preach to the children; that would have been making them serve a particular area of his teaching gift. Instead he gave them what they needed, a knee to sit on. He didn't question Mary's faith as she cried over Lazarus, he just wept with her and then raised Lazarus from the dead afterwards. Why? Because in those few moments Mary just needed a shoulder to cry on. His shoulder became a gift to her, meeting her right where she was at.

Jesus was the ultimate example of a consumed life. His whole life was about serving others and he gave it away willingly. Mark says, *'Jesus did not come to be served but to serve, and to give his life as a ransom for many'.*[2] What an incredible verse which so many in God's House seem to have missed. If Jesus, our Lord and master did not come to be served, then why should his people go to his House expecting room service? The consumers in the House are infatuated with being served and have forgotten that their purpose is the same as Christ's; they must live to give.

The House of God is supposed to be an accurate representation of Jesus. It should be a place where everyone who walks through its door leaves carrying gifts. It should be a place where the gifts of belonging, safety, wisdom, and the gift of a warm welcome are given away freely to all. This spirit of the giver needs to be restored to the House of God.

Here are some things I believe we must put into practice to ensure that as a church, we are operating as a gift to the world.

A GIFT IS NOT EARNED

Many Houses have stopped giving their life away and instead, only respond to needs in their surrounding community if they are given a good enough reason to do so. They don't volunteer to get involved with hurting humanity and are not willing to embrace a dying world. Maybe that's because life subliminally teaches us that gifts are to be earned. So, if you make it through another year, you get a birthday or anniversary gift. When you graduate college or pass your driving test, you get cards and gifts of congratulation.

The Message Bible says: *'If you're a hard worker and you do a good job, you deserve your pay; we don't call your wages a gift.'*[3] In other words, each month when you get paid, you aren't surprised because you have earned it. Your salary is owed to you. The language of 'gift' only comes to the fore when we move to the matter of serving and blessing people in situations where they did not earn it. Indeed, the most treasured gifts are those you receive totally out of the blue, you just were not expecting them, but someone decided to bless your world.

FOR NO REASON

The House of God must be a place that gives away all it has without expecting anything in return. In your family home do people have to earn forgiveness, acceptance, a second chance or your love? No. And neither must we allow this thinking to infiltrate our churches. If it does, we will soon have people who do not tithe unless there is a good reason, do not worship unless God has blessed them and who are unwilling to serve unless the pastor has impressed them.

I don't remember earning my forgiveness. I don't remember earning the second chance Christ gave me through the cross. But God gave me one anyway. What about you? Every day I tell my husband Steve that I love him. Sometimes he will ask, 'Why?' And I will always reply, 'No reason!' That's not because I can't think of one, there are many reasons why I love him. The point is I don't ever want to make my love for him dependent on a list of reasons because that means he has to earn my love. And if there are reasons why he earns it, then for those same reasons I can take my love away. Be careful if people in your House start to make their love dependant on reasons. They are not loving the House, they are controlling it, and your House will never be able to grow beyond their permissions.

Take a moment to read Luke 6:27-38. This passage will test whether or not you have grasped this principle, and indicate whether or not our Houses are a true reflection of God's heart. It asks us to love our enemies, to give the person who steals our coat a gift-wrapped tunic as well! It teaches us to love people for no reason. The final verse says, *'Give and it will be given to you, pressed down, shaken together and running over.'*[4] I have heard this verse quoted many times but rarely in its true context. The context is one of loving your enemies. If we want a House that is blessed to the point of overflow then we need to sort our love life out. Are those who have stolen from you welcomed back into your House? Can those who have hurt you and criticised the House find a place of restoration and forgiveness? Is your House one that embraces the prodigals and those who have betrayed it and squandered its blessings?

YOUR HOUSE WILL PICK UP THE BILL

Something else we must understand about the nature of a gift is that you are supposed to pick up the bill. When you buy someone a gift, you pay. You don't walk up to your friend and say, 'It's your birthday next week, so give me £50 and I will buy you something nice.' No, you are supposed to pay for it out of your own resources and then remove the price tag so the person who receives this gift is unaware of how much it cost you.

Sometimes the things you go through in order to build God's House are costly. We are taught from an early age that expensive things need to be handled with care. We are told they are not for every day use, like that new pair of trainers you desperately want to wear for school but Mum says they are only for special occasions. But God is not like that. He wants you to take those things that have cost you dearly and give them away freely to others in the House. When you build the House of God you will have to build through times of difficulty, you will have to build through times of opposition, you will have to build through times of lack. But all those experiences are the price tag which no one is supposed to see. Be provoked by the Macedonian churches about whose giving Paul said: *'Out of severe trial came overflowing joy and out of extreme poverty came rich generosity'.*[5] That church had learned the power of giving.

THE GIFT IS TO BE BEAUTIFULLY WRAPPED

The way a gift is presented is very important to me. Any woman will tell you that a bunch of flowers from the petrol station, which were a last minute thought and half dead anyway, do not mean as much as the flowers that were hand-picked for you at the florist. Imagine you were allowed to choose between two gifts. One is wrapped in newspaper with a tatty piece of string holding it together. The other is wrapped in beautiful gold paper. It is tied with expensive looking ribbon and has a pretty gift tag with your name on. The gift inside both packages is the same but one speaks of care, love, time, thought and preparation. The other speaks of last minute convenience. For too long the House of God has taken the most amazing gift the world has ever seen and wrapped it shabbily without due thought, care or attention. As a result, many people fail to be consumed by God's House because of our tatty wrapping!

Over the past few years our church has attracted an increasing amount of interest from the secular media. What has brought them to our House is the way we have 'gift wrapped' Christ. On every occasion, whether the visitor was the BBC, ITV or a national newspaper they all walked away saying the same thing, 'I didn't know church could be like this!' They walked away breathless, like the Queen of Sheba did after she visited the House Solomon had built. They came expecting God's House to be cold, stark, uninviting and certainly not a place they could imagine going to themselves. They now take away the impression that God's House is magnificent and a place they could belong. That is exactly what we want them to think because it gives them a true reflection of who the owner is. God never does anything poorly. He never does anything without care and consideration, nor does he scrimp and save to put the next event on. He certainly doesn't live in a run down shack. It's time we stopped giving people this impression of God's House.

An Excellent Gift

Excellence is something I am passionate about but too many people think excellence only belongs to those who have a large budget. They say, 'If I had the money your church has, then of course we would be excellent.' But that excuse isn't acceptable because excellence isn't about a budget, it's about a spirit. Excellence is about approaching everything you do with an attitude that wants to make the most out of everything that God has entrusted to your care.

When we were first married and moved into our new home, I decorated it excellently. I did the best with what we had. I didn't have enough money to re-carpet the house but I could afford to hire a sander, so we did the floors. We couldn't afford to wallpaper everywhere but I could afford a tin of paint to repaint the walls. Too often we say, 'Well I can't afford to do it' and simply do nothing. If you want to get to the place where you have a big budget, start maximising what you have today. Stop burying your talent in the ground and start investing it.[6]

A House not a museum

The excellence that we have at Abundant Life is not only visible, it is tangible; you can touch it and feel it. Our House is excellent in appearance but it is not a museum, it is a work place. You will not find 'Do not touch' signs all around our House. God wants an excellence that says to everyone who walks through the doors of his House, 'Welcome, we prepared all this for you.'

My parents once went to view a house that was for sale. They were greeted at the other side of the huge electronic gates by a very proud homeowner. Their viewing experience then began to go downhill when they were asked to put on blue plastic covers over their own shoes, to protect the hand dyed wool carpets. The owner then proceeded to explain how to care for the marble floors and how the ornate fountain in the centre of the entrance lobby must never be turned onto full power to prevent the water splashing onto its granite surround and leaving stains. He then explained how to clean the gold dolphin shaped taps and take care of the hand painted ceilings over the swimming pool. And so the list went on, listened to by my bored parents who after first encountering the fountain and the taps knew this house was not for them! The proud owner was so infatuated with the excellence of his furnishings that the house had ceased to be a home; it was more like a museum. He didn't speak about the house with any affection or talk about the happy memories he and his wife had while living there. The tour was about maintenance and the importance of keeping the upholstery clean. The house even had a completely separate wing for his children and grandchildren to use when they visited, which of course had no expensive decorations they could damage.

As my parents told of their forty-minute agony, being bored senseless by this man's monologue of information, my thoughts turned to God's House. Although we should always aim for excellence we must never mistake it for opulence. Having excellence in God's House isn't just about the décor and equipment, it is about the spirit and heart attitude of the people living there.

WE DID ALL THIS FOR YOU

I will never forget the first time I visited Mercy Ministries in Nashville, USA. It's a home that was founded by an incredible lady called Nancy Alcorn who I am privileged to count as a friend. Nancy built a home to help hurting, damaged young women get their lives back on track. The Mercy House looks after the girls free of charge. It is a gift Nancy has given them with the price tag removed. When I walked through the doors of that home I cried. It was completely overwhelming as I imagined what a hurt, scared young girl fleeing a life of abuse and drugs would think when they walked through those doors for the first time. They would be completely amazed because you are not faced by a hostile, stark, half way house. It is more like walking through the front door of a top hotel. There was beautiful artwork on the walls, a galleried balcony with large arched windows. The lounge was beautifully decorated with rich warm fabrics and each bedroom was en-suite. Many of these girls who had been told all their lives that they didn't deserve nice things, were entering God's House to be told, 'you are the reason we have done this – welcome home!'

Every few months, here at Abundant Life Church we hold special VIP banquets. These are amazing days that everyone loves being a part of. Our sole purpose on the day is to lavish love and excellence on the people that we are reaching, people who may be homeless, in prostitution, battling with drug addictions or trying to escape a life of crime. On that day we hire in shower blocks and people from the church come and give their professional expertise to serve our VIP guests. We have doctors, dentists, chiropodists, beauticians and hairdressers. Each guest is given a personal makeover including a health check and a new hairstyle. This is completed by a visit to our dressing room where they can choose an outfit of their choice from racks of quality, donated clothing. Tailors and seamstresses are on hand to make the necessary alterations to make their new clothes fit them perfectly. We then escort them down a red carpet to a candlelit four-course dinner, where the tables are waited on by our consumed volunteers.

This is our way of saying, 'We are doing this for you, everything in God's House is here for you to enjoy!' There are few dry eyes as people look at their reflection in the mirror and for the first time in many years see a new person looking back. These same people arrived with their head hung low and with their sleeping bag under their arm. But they were embraced by the excellence of our House and that embrace gave them a glimpse of what their future could look like. In that moment they begin to dare to dream again about a different life. The VIP banquets don't just give them a meal or a new suit of clothes, but restore their hope and dignity. You can witness some of these amazing transformations for yourself on the DVD at the back of this book.

Recently we had some items stolen from one of our offices. We later found out it was someone we had fed at one of our free breakfasts. What happened next was amazing. Some of the other homeless people we had already reached out to, went and found the culprit. They brought him back along with the stolen goods and asked for our forgiveness. The excellence of the House had made them feel differently about themselves and they did not want to steal or misuse that excellence. They realised that there were no 'Do not touch' signs in our House because we were already willing to share everything we had and use it to bless their world. They now wanted to protect the excellence of the House they had enjoyed.

By wrapping up the gift of God's House with excellence, and by making it look attractive to the world, you send a clear signal out about the value your House places on this gift. The House we are building is to be given, not forced, and not pushed upon people. We are simply to open the doors and let them see the beauty inside and the rest is up to them. But if we are building a House like I have tried to describe in this book, then I can guarantee that people will find it irresistible.

THIS GIFT OPENS DOORS

I sometimes look at my life and ask, 'How did I end up here? How have I managed to be only thirty-one yet doing some amazing things and living my dream?' I cannot point to many big moments along the way, just lots of small 'no one sees' moments where I became consumed with zeal for God's House. I have discovered that, *'a gift opens the way for the giver and ushers him into the presence of the great.'*[7] Notice who this gift opens the way for: the giver! If you want your House to be given new doors of favour, opportunity and blessing, then give. If today this book finds you striving to build something that will get you noticed, if you are trying to bypass the work of preparation and force what God is clearly not endorsing, then it is time to stop living as a consumer and let zeal for his House consume your life.

PAT'S STORY

'Because I was planted in God's House,
I survived. And I know I will continue to thrive
as I now pour my life back into the lives of
broken and hurting people.'

I was adopted as a baby and was brought up by a strict Catholic mother. My father did not practise any religion. I went to Catholic schools and was taught to fear God and learned about the different sizes of sins and about purgatory. I left church at 14 having decided in my heart that God did not exist. As a teenager I was very rebellious.

Twenty years later I became a Christian at a Billy Graham crusade. At the time I was living with my partner Richard. We had a daughter, Chantelle, who was 8. I also had an older daughter, Mandy, who was 19 and had left home.

After I became a Christian I really felt we needed to get married and I needed to put things right with Richard. He had always wanted to get married but I did not want to because of past hurts and insecurities. We got married quickly and quietly in the registry office – we thought that best because Richard was not a Christian.

By this time I was at college training to be a nurse. I was 36 and having been told that I could not have any more children, I decided I would have a career. Much to my doctor's amazement I got pregnant within ten weeks of getting married!

I was still a relatively new Christian and had been 'church hopping' for a year or so. This taught me a lot of things but I could not settle anywhere. As I was praying about which church to settle at, I had to drive Richard a new route to work for two weeks. Each morning I passed a building on the hill with a sign 'Abundant Life Centre'. I had never heard of it but I felt a sort of magnetic pull towards the building.

All I can say is that when I went in I had already seen it in a dream! I knew this was the place God had brought me to. Two weeks later I got baptised there and Richard came to watch. At the time he smoked heavily and did not think he could ever stop but after my baptism he never smoked again;

the desire went completely. He knew God was on his case and became a Christian nine months later.

I had a son, Kelvin, and when he was 8 months old I fell pregnant again. I was very ill. My doctor advised me to have a termination because I had lost so much blood and because of my history of stillbirth, I was scared. I was 38 and pregnant with a lot of health problems, but I knew I could not abort the baby.

When Natasha was born, she had a solid knot in her umbilical cord. The doctor who saw it said: 'Someone upstairs is looking after you'. He brought all the students in to look at the knot and he said he did not know how any oxygen had got through it. So we had three children in the house, Chantelle aged 11, Kelvin 18 months, and newborn Natasha.

For the next five years we got stuck into the church and got on with our lives until one awful day when my beautiful, precious daughter Chantelle, suddenly died. She had been babysitting with a group of friends and they sniffed some lighter fuel for a laugh. She collapsed and died. It was the worst day of my life. I could not put into words what this did to me. All I can say, six and a half years later, is that God brought me and my family through it. Mandy, my eldest daughter, became a Christian and is now in the Church along with many others who gave their lives to God because of Chantelle's sudden death.

Around that time I met many people who had also lost children but who had never moved on. Some were visiting their child's grave every day; others were involved in Spiritualism. I think God showed me these people to help me see that I had a choice to make. I could be like them, or just trust him.

I did of course have to grieve and I felt I would never be the same again. It was like losing a leg and having to learn to walk in a different way. But as I started to study scriptures about heaven, God revealed things to me, not in a weird way, but through books and the people around me in God's House. I realise now that Chantelle is in a great place. No harm can come to her and she is so happy. I know I will always miss her but because I know I will see her again, I have made a decision to just trust God.

I received so much love and support when Chantelle died, both practically and spiritually. I did not cook at all for well over a month and people were available for us even in the middle of the night. I don't know what I'd have done if I had not been firmly planted in God's House.

I also got busy helping to build the House of God. We launched the Chantelle Bleau Memorial Fund, a ministry established in her name to educate children about the dangers of solvent abuse. I also started reaching out to other hurting women, such as those fleeing violence, involved in prostitution or with addictions. I kept moving the focus off how terrible I felt and onto other people's pain. I saw that many people have been through far worse things than me and as I reached out to them, my asthma, panic attacks and skin disorder all disappeared. I'd also put on a lot of weight through comfort eating but that went as well.

For about two years after Chantelle's death, when I went to significant events like weddings or concerts I would feel totally drained. At the church's Christmas Cabaret event I remember watching one of her friends sing and I could not help thinking that Chantelle should have been there on the stage too. The pain was unbearable and I thought I was going to pass out. But whenever this happened a warm tangible presence surrounded me, holding me up, and I heard God whisper 'she's with me and there is no place and no love better than mine'.

Today I feel very much stronger in my faith than I did before Chantelle left us and I really thank God that I was grounded in such a good solid Church with such strong, wise people around me. Because I was planted in God's House, I survived. And I know I will continue to thrive as I now pour my life back into the lives of broken and hurting people who need to know the love of our good God and the friendship of his wonderful people.

Pat

Pat Bleau

THANK YOU

While writing this book, hundreds of faces and thousands of lives have flashed through the corridors of my mind. At times I have wept as I have thought about the sacrifice that some have made to build the House of God. So as I close this book I want to speak from the heart of God to every person who has made the decision to move from being a consumer in God's House to being consumed.

For every hour that you have given in service to the House, for every sacrifice you have made for the sake of the House, for every hurt you have hidden in order not to damage the House, for every night you have laid awake praying for the House, for every life you have embraced, for every word of encouragement you have spoken in the House, the heart of God says 'thank you'.

You have loved what he loves, you have cared when others didn't and you have cherished his House more than your own. For you there is a special touch of heaven because those who lose their lives gain even more.[8] I celebrate and salute every fellow zealot in the House. Between us we can build a home that God wants to dwell in and we can be sure that any future generation who look through the keyholes of our churches will know exactly who lives in a House like this!

'Is it a time for you yourselves to be living in your panelled houses while this House remains a ruin? Give careful thought to your ways. Go up into the mountains and bring down timber and build the house, so I may take pleasure in it and be honoured, says the Lord.'[9]

[1] John 3:16
[2] Mark 10:45
[3] Romans 4:4
[4] Luke 6:38
[5] 2 Corinthians 8:2
[6] Matthew 25:18, 26-27
[7] Proverbs 18:16
[8] Matthew 10:39
[9] Haggai 1:4, 7-8

DEAR CHILD

FOR EVERY HOUR THAT YOU HAVE GIVEN IN SERVICE TO THE HOUSE, FOR EVERY SACRIFICE YOU HAVE MADE FOR THE SAKE OF THE HOUSE, FOR EVERY HURT YOU HAVE HIDDEN IN ORDER NOT TO DAMAGE THE HOUSE, FOR EVERY NIGHT YOU HAVE LAID AWAKE PRAYING FOR THE HOUSE, FOR EVERY LIFE YOU HAVE EMBRACED, FOR EVERY ENCOURAGEMENT YOU HAVE SPOKEN IN THE HOUSE, THE HEART OF GOD SAYS

'THANK YOU'

You are so welcome to join us for any of our services:
Abundant Life Church
Wapping Road, Bradford, West Yorkshire, England

Service times: Sunday 10.30am and 6pm
Wednesday 7.30pm

We are committed to building God's House and to helping every other consumed builder. We host several annual conferences, which exist to train those in God's House. For more information on these events just visit **www.alm.org.uk**

Build the House - *March*
These are one-day training events for leaders in the house with word ministry from Pastor Paul Scanlon and Pastor Charlotte Scanlon-Gambill.

Devoted - *April*
Hosted by Pastor Lara Martin

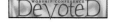

A training event for worship teams with workshops on all aspects of building a thriving worship team to strengthen the local church.

Cherish - *June*

Hosted by Pastor Charlotte Scanlon-Gambill
Our annual women's conference. This is a 3-day event with awesome worship and powerful word ministry from Charlotte and other key speakers. Come and be cherished!

RockNations - *August*
Hosted by Pastor Steve Gambill
A summer camp designed to help young people flourish. This event exists to equip the next generation. Four days of intense activities, extreme worship and word ministry.

Stronger - *September*
Hosted by the Abundant Life Church leadership team

An event for the whole family, from senior pastors to community workers there is something for everyone. Stronger is the heartbeat of our consumed church and will give you a behind the scenes look at how we are building church in the 21st century.

Xcel - *November*
Hosted by Pastor Paul Scanlon
A conference for men only. Two days of inspiring ministry to help men excel in every area of life.

Full details of other resources by
Charlotte Scanlon-Gambill are available from:

Abundant Life Church
Wapping Road, Bradford
West Yorkshire BD3 0EQ

Tel: +44 (0)1274 307233
Fax: +44 (0)1274 740698
Email: admin@alm.org.uk

For a copy of our free quarterly magazine 'Voice to the Nations'
please contact us as above.

Visit our online store at www.alm.org.uk

Browse the full range of preaching, teaching, training, music
and worship resources available from Abundant Life Ministries

---

Other book titles available from
Abundant Life Resources:

It's Not Over 'Till The Barren Woman Sings
by Paul Scanlon

Crossing Over
by Paul Scanlon

The Battle For The Loins
by Paul Scanlon

THIS DVD IS A WINDOW INTO THE LIFE OF THE ABUNDANT LIFE CHURCH, BRADFORD. ON IT YOU WILL SEE SOME OF THE PEOPLE REFERRED TO IN THIS BOOK AND MANY OTHERS WHO ARE CONSUMED WITH A SIMILAR PASSION TO BUILD THIS 21ST CENTURY CHURCH AND IMPACT OUR COMMUNITY.

21st Century Church -
Looking through the keyhole of Abundant Life Church
A look through the keyhole to see what church in the 21st Century can look like when it's built with a zeal for God's House that consumes us.

Restoration Trust -
Listening through the keyhole of Abundant Life Church
The heartbeat of Abundant Life Church is to restore hope and dignity to broken lives and Restoration Trust is our vehicle for doing this. This inner city ministry exists to help those searching for a place of safety and belonging to discover that God's House can be their home.

As For Me -
The sound of praise
This track from our recent album 'How Loved' expresses the desire of every consumed heart:
> 'There is no other place that I would rather be,
> Than in you House, its where I'm meant to be.
> Here I can fly and here my dreams can live, I have decided...'